MW00788790

Submitted for your perusal...

Trivia from
The Twilight Zone

Bill DeVóe

A delightful compendium of word search puzzles,
photo quizzes, match games, chaser quizzes, a jumbo
crossword puzzle and much more – all from one
of the greatest television shows ever produced.

Acknowledgements

Thanks and admiration to Carol Serling, Anne Francis,
Jean Carson, Wright King, Phillip Pine, Don Keefer,
Barbara Stuart, Ruta Lee, Cliff Robertson, Russell Johnson,
Suzanne LLoyd, Paul Comi, Arlene Martel, Ann Jillian,
Shelley Fabares, Theodore Bikel, Kevin McCarthy and Ivan Dixon.

Special thanks to Andrew Ramage, Stewart Stanyard, Tony
Albarella, Dwight Deskins, Matthew Cregg and Ben Ohmart.

. . . and to my wonderful family for enduring
countless hours of Twilight Zone re-runs and
my bad Rod Serling impersonations.

Trivia from The Twilight Zone
© 2004 B. DeVóe. All Rights Reserved.

The photographic images contained in this book are the property of CBS/Viacom. Portions of this book appeared in Rod Serling's The Twilight Zone Magazine Special Edition; Trivia from Rod Serling's The Twilight Zone. The Twilight Zone is a copyrighted franchise of CBS/Viacom.

All illustrations are copyright of their respective owners, and are also reproduced here in the spirit of publicity. Whilst we have made every effort to acknowledge specific credits whenever possible, we apologize for any omissions, and will undertake every effort to make any appropriate changes in future editions of this book if necessary.

No part of this book may be reproduced in any form or by any means, electronic, mechanical, digital, photocopying or recording, except for the inclusion in a review, without permission in writing from the publisher.

Published in the USA by:
BearManor Media
P O Box 71426
Albany, Georgia 31708
www.bearmanormedia.com

ISBN 1-59393-136-0

Printed in the United States of America.

Book design by Darlene Swanson of Van-garde Imagery, Inc.

Contents:

Associate Level of Twilight Zone Knowledge 11

Master Level of Twilight Zone Knowledge. 69

Master Level of Twilight Zone Knowledge Answers 125

Associate Level of Twilight Zone Knowledge

Th_his Section will introduce you to some of the more familiar facts associated with the greatest television series ever created ... The Twilight Zone.

At the same time however, don't be surprised if you're suddenly exposed to some baffling befuddlements, perplexing puzzlers, or questionable queries.

Submitted for your enjoyment ...

Associate Level of Twilight Zone Knowledge

For Starters:

Warm up with these ten True or False Teasers found only in The Twilight Zone.

1.	*The Twilight Zone* was originally filmed in color.	T	F
2.	*The Twilight Zone* enjoyed a five-year run.	T	F
3.	Desi Arnaz was originally contracted to narrate the series.	T	F
4.	During the second season, 6 episodes were videotaped to save money.	T	F
5.	Burgess Meredith and Jack Klugman each starred in 4 episodes.	T	F

6.	*The Twilight Zone* was replaced in 1964 by Bonanza.	T	F
7.	Steven Spielberg began his career as a director on Serling's *Night Gallery*.	T	F
8.	*The Twilight Zone* expanded to an hour in its fourth season.	T	F
9.	You can now buy *Twilight Zone* trading cards.	T	F
10.	Carol Serling acted as Associate Publisher of *Twilight Zone Magazine*.	T	F

Sounds And Silences

Fill in the blanks to complete Rod Serling's opening narration:

"You're traveling _____ another _____
              (1)   (2)

a dimension not only of _____ and sound but
                              (3)

of mind; a journey into a _____ land whose
                          (4)

_____ are that of _____.
    (5)   (6)

That's the _____ up ahead – your next
                    (7)

_____ The Twilight Zone!"
    (8)

Patterns

Unscramble these seven one-word Twilight Zone titles

1.	TASICT
2.	WOT
3.	SDTU
4.	GLEYE
5.	EETCXUNOI
6.	TEMU
7.	ELETS

TZ Fact:

Did you know that Rod Serling sometimes found inspiration for his stories by walking the backlot at MGM?

Picture If You Will

Which one of these images is not from the Twilight Zone opening montage?

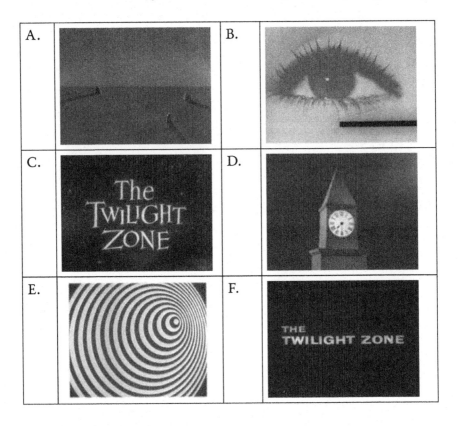

Where Is Everybody?

Find the names, places, words and objects hidden in the puzzle

H	A	N	P	N	O	I	S	N	E	M	I	D	H	T	F	I	F	A	J	S
T	I	U	S	D	V	O	P	S	R	U	N	N	S	T	U	U	Z	A	D	A
I	T	T	R	T	A	F	A	F	T	E	R	H	O	U	R	S	R	D	E	Y
H	T	I	C	V	V	A	B	R	A	P	A	S	S	A	N	R	U	O	E	B
E	D	Q	U	H	G	E	Z	D	O	D	N	O	P	D	E	S	I	L	N	H
U	S	A	R	T	H	G	O	P	O	R	H	U	A	N	T	E	K	L	A	G
Q	T	O	L	O	J	I	P	W	D	V	O	M	R	D	E	A	T	H	B	U
U	I	D	L	A	D	B	K	G	O	A	B	P	D	I	L	O	P	A	P	O
P	M	D	O	W	O	S	Y	E	C	H	N	I	W	R	O	C	Z	O	N	L
D	E	M	N	V	O	M	E	E	R	D	J	P	D	A	S	I	L	V	R	L
R	O	D	D	Z	P	O	R	R	Z	O	N	D	A	R	B	E	M	I	S	I
E	H	W	T	H	E	T	W	I	L	I	G	H	T	Z	O	N	E	W	P	W
A	H	P	R	J	L	O	O	P	N	I	H	C	T	I	W	E	B	T	S	R
M	A	I	U	Q	U	S	T	I	M	A	N	A	K	A	G	J	L	D	G	G
P	I	N	M	A	A	C	N	U	S	T	H	G	I	N	D	I	M	O	D	D
N	Y	A	P	C	T	E	M	P	L	E	T	O	N	B	R	I	R	E	N	D
J	A	M	E	S	O	N	S	E	M	E	K	N	D	P	Y	Q	N	I	N	O
M	D	O	T	D	B	Z	A	T	L	E	V	J	O	Y	X	V	R	G	A	O
F	S	V	U	D	E	I	L	G	N	I	L	W	O	H	S	I	Z	T	L	W
S	M	E	C	V	H	O	N	N	B	Z	X	D	F	K	L	S	G	S	E	E
D	O	E	S	D	X	A	W	U	G	L	C	I	N	V	A	D	E	R	S	M
G	O	V	F	G	R	Z	F	O	Y	K	A	A	K	M	J	W	H	Y	I	O
A	D	A	R	C	O	R	N	F	I	E	L	D	E	L	E	T	Z	O	N	H

1. Long Live Walter _____.

2. He stalked Lew Bookman and Nan Adams.

3. The _____, third season episode starring Lois Nettleton.

4. Henry_____, Serling's Santa.

5. The _____ Of Flight 33

6. In Praise Of ____.

7. Hungry visitors from To Serve Man

8. The _____ Man, second season episode with John Carradine.

9. Martin Sloan's boyhood town.

10. Nick Of _____, William Shatner's first episode.

11. _____ Play, second season episode starring Dennis Weaver.

12. A Stop At _____.

13. "That's the signpost up ahead – your next stop, _____.

14. Where Anthony Fremont put those who thought bad thoughts.

15. The instrument Klugman played in his first Twilight Zone episode.

16. Perchance To _____.

17. Twilight Zone creator.

18. Henry _____, Serling's bookworm banker

19. The _____, first season episode starring Anne Francis.

20. The _____, first season episode starring Inger Stevens

21. Oliver _____, two feet tall.

22. The Eye Of The _____.

23. Mr. Denton On _____.

24. The _____, Twilight Zone's final episode.

25. Mr. _____, The Strong, Burgess Meredith's second episode.

26. The _____, classic episode starring Agnes Moorehead.

27. The Trouble With _____, Brian Aherne's starring role.

28. Living _____, fifth season episode starring Telly Savalas.

29. "There is a _____, (opening narration).

30. The _____ Man, second season episode with Burgess Meredith and Fritz Weaver.

More Sounds And Silences

Fill in the blanks to complete Rod Serling's opening narration.

"You unlock this _____ With the key of
_____ Beyond it is another _____ . . .
    (2)   (3)
a dimension of _____ . . . a dimension of
    (4)
_____ . . . a dimension of _____
    (5)   (6)
You're moving into a _____ of both _____
    (7)   (8)
and substance, of things and _____ You've just
    (9)
_____ over into the _____ Zone".
    (10)   (11)

Synonymically-Speaking

Unscramble these synonyms to find the correct Twilight Zone title

1. The Enormous Elevated Inclination   a. Death Ship

2. The Antiquated Mortal   b. The Jeopardy Room

3. Feasible Fantasy   c. Night of the Meek

4. The Perilous Chamber   d. The Obsolete Man

5. Canyon Of The Specter   e. A Quality of Mercy

6. A Condition Of Benevolence   f. Valley Of The Shadow

7. Expired Orbiter   g. The Big Tall Wish

8. The Undiminished Accuracy   h. The Man In The Bottle

9. Twilight Of The Tame   i. Perchance To Dream

10. The Dude In The Decanter   j. The Whole Truth

A Short Drink . . .

It's Happy-Hour in the Twilight Zone. Match up the characters on the
right with their drink of choice.

1. Ginger Ale	a. Mr. Smith (The Devil)
2. Irish Whiskey	b. Ione Sykes
3. Double Martini	c. Mr. Dundee
4. Chocolate Ice Cream Soda	d. Rance McGrew
5. Red Eye	e. Valerie #8, Lana Cuberlee #12
6. Tequila with a cube of sugar	f. Dave Gurney
7. Instant Smile	g. Martin Sloan
8. Ice Coffee	h. McNulty & Potts
9. Beer	i. Dane, Nate Bledsoe
10. Cherry Brandy (vintage 1903)	j. Don & Pat Carter

A Little TZ Q & A

Question: Why is this man so happy?		Answer:
Question: Why is this woman in the hospital?		Answer:
Question: What does this man have under his cap?		Answer:
Question: What is this man looking at?		Answer:

From Boss To Blockhead
Match the supervisor on the left with the subordinate on the right.

1. Mr. Dundee	a. Mr. Armbruster
2. Mr. Cooper	b. Henry Bemis
3. Mr. Misrell	c. Henry Corwin
4. Mr. Cosgrove	d. Horace Ford
5. Mr. Judson	e. Bob Frazier
6. Mr. Bagby	f. Agnes Grep
7. Mr. Peabody	g. Patrick Thomas McNulty
8. Mr. Sloan	h. Charley Parkes
9. Mr. Stout	i. Hector B Poole
10. Mr. V.C Diemel	j. Gart Williams

– Bonus Quiz –

The Chaser (Part I)
Let's play 20 questions Twilight Zone style!

1. Why does Rocky Valentine ask Pip to furnish him with a new automobile?

2. Name the two stars that starred in Two.

3. In The Chaser, Roger Shakleforth buys two potions. What is the name of the second potion?

4. In The Bewitchin' Pool, who do Jeb and Sport find when they jump into their swimming pool?

5. What radio station helps Ed Lindsey recapture the past?

6. What second season episode co-stars Don Rickles?

7. In what episode does Jack the Ripper make a chilling appearance?

8. Name The Twilight Zone's first episode.

9. In The Grave, how much does Johnny Rob bet Conny Miller that he won't visit the grave of Pinto Sykes?

10. In The Howling Man, whom does David Ellington release from the hermitage?

11. In The Rip Van Winkle Caper, how long do Farwell and his cohorts remain in suspended animation?

12. In what two episodes can you find Martin Landau?

13. In The Fever, what does Franklin find waiting outside the door of his hotel room?

14. In Mirror Image, how does Paul Grinstead get the bus depot?

15. In what episode can you find Martin Milner?

16. In The Sixteen-Millimeter Shrine, who was Barbara Jean's leading man in A Night In Paris?

17. In A Game Of Pool, what are the stakes that Jesse and Fats agree to?

18. Who's "not bad" at aggies?

19. In what classic episode can you hear the less-than-musical question, "Anthony, are you making it snow?"

20. In what three episodes can you find Morgan Brittany?

TZ Fact:

Did you know that a vintage Twilight Zone board game by IDEAL recently sold on ebay for over $200.00?

Fame And Misfortune

Which of the following famous people was never portrayed on The Twilight Zone?
    a. William Shakespeare
    b. Julius Caesar
    c. Abraham Lincoln
    d. Adolf Hitler

The Thirty Fathom Grave

Which of the following ships never graced the murky waters of The Twilight Zone?
    a. The Lady Anne
    b. The Lusitania
    c. S.S. Queen Of Glasgow
    d. The Titanic

The Mind And The Matter

Name the common objects that complete these Twilight Zone titles.

1. A Kind Of _____

2. A Most Unusual _____

3. Dead Man's _____

4. _____ Image

5. The Man In The _____

6. Kick The _____

7. A _____ For Your Thoughts

8. What's In The _____

The Silence

Which of the following actors never appeared in a Twilight Zone episode?

a. Arte Johnson

b. Bill Bixby

c. Jim Nabors

d. Jack Albertson

e. Martin Balsam

Which of the following actresses never appeared in a Twilight Zone episode?

    a. Cloris Leachman

    b. Rita Moreno

    c. Mariette Hartley

    d. Shelley Fabares

    e. Ann Blyth

Crime And Comeuppance

Simply match these characters as they appeared in various episodes.

What's Mine Is Mine

Match the item on the left with the rightful owner

1. automobile account   a. Julie Baines
2. bomb shelter   b. Comfort Gatewood
3. country blue's record   c. Paul Radin
4. pearl hairpin   d. Dan Hollis
5. paintings   e. Johnny-Rob
6. twenty-dollar gold piece   f. Pamela Morris
7. medicinal bandage   g. Jess-Belle
8. Scarabaeid Beetle   h. Norma
9. ham radio set   i. Jake Ross
10. Perry Como album   j. Steve Brand

Still More Sounds and Silences

Fill in the blanks to complete Rod Serling's opening narration.

"There is a _____ dimension beyond that which
              (1)

_____ to man. It is a dimension _____ as
       (2)   (3)

_____ and as timeless as _____.
       (4)   (5)

It is the middle ground between _____
                                        (6)

and shadow, between science and _____,
                                        (7)

and it lies between the _____ of man's
                                (8)

fears and the _____ of his _____.
                    (9)   (10)

This is the dimension of _____. It is an area which
                                (11)

we _____ The Twilight _____ .
         (12)   (13)

A Thing About Numbers

Fill in the blanks to compete these numerical Twilight Zone titles.

1. The _____ Is Made Up of Phantoms

2. _____ For The Angels

3. The _____ Millimeter Shrine

4. King _____ Will Not Return

5. The Odyssey Of Flight _____

6. _____ From The Sun

7. The _____ Of Us Are Dying

8. Nervous Man In A _____ Dollar Room

9. A _____ Yards Over The Rim

10. _____ Characters In Search Of An Exit

11. _____ O'Clock

12. The _____ -Fathom Grave

13. Nightmare At _____ Feet

14. Number _____ Looks Just Like You

15. Probe _____ Over And Out

16. _____ Years Without Slumbering

-Bonus Quiz-

The Chaser (Part. II)

1. In A Hundred Yards Over The Rim, what does Christian Horn bring back to the wagon upon returning from the future?

2. What is the maximum amount of experiments allowed by the State in The Eye Of The Beholder?

3. In Hocus-Pocus And Frisby, what does Frisby use to escape from the aliens?

4. In Five Characters In Search Of An Exit, where does the Major assume they are trapped?

5. What is significant about the number 6708777?

6. In Mr. Bevis, what is year and make of Orson Bean's car?

7. Where was Artie Beechcroft killed?

8. In It's A Good Life, how many bottles of whiskey are left?

9. In The Big Tall Wish, where does Bolie Jackson's comeback take place?

10. Who was disconnected, discombooberated and behind in her rent?

11. Name the four episodes scripted by George Clayton Johnson.

12. Which actor played a musician, a pool shark, a spaceship captain and a bookie in his four starring roles on The Twilight Zone?

13. What musical instrument does Floyd Burney play?

14. In what episode can you find a very young Ron Howard?

15. In The Mirror, how does Clemente kill D'Allesandro?

16. In The Fear, what was Miss Scott's profession?

17. What actor played a bank teller, a vacuum cleaner salesman, a librarian, and the Devil in his four starring roles on The Twilight Zone?

18. In Night Of The Meek, what does Percival Smithers want for Christmas?

19. In Escape Clause, how does Bedeker's wife die?

20. What is the name of the script that Booth Templeton brings back form the speakeasy?

TZ Speak:

"It was an honor to do a Twilight Zone."
      . . . Shelly Fabares (Black Leather Jackets)

Bachelor Level of Twilight Zone Knowledge

This Section raises the bar by throwing in some twisted teasers, entangling entrapments and confusing conundrums.

So roll up your sleeves, sharpen your pencils and dive in!

Submitted for your enjoyment . . .

Bachelor Level of Twilight Zone Knowledge

Pleased To Present Mr. Rod Serling

Name the episodes in which Rod Serling can be heard saying:

1. Cameo of a man who has just lost his most valuable possession."
   a) *Little Girl Lost*
   b) *Person Or Person's Unknown*
   c) *Static*

2. "Picture of a woman looking at a picture."
   a) *The Sixteen-Millimeter Shrine*
   b) *The Hunt*
   c) *The Passersby*

3. "You walk into this room at you own risk."
   a) *Time Enough At Last*
   b) *The Shelter*
   c) *The Obsolete Man*

4. "It may be said with a degree of assurance that not everything that meets the eye is as it appears."
   a) *The Mirror*
   b) *The Long Morrow*
   c) *Mirror Image*

5. "This is one of the out-of-the-way places."
   a) *The Invaders*
   b) *A Nice Place to Visit*
   c) *Third From The Sun*

6. Name the only two episodes in which Rod Serling announces the title of the episode in the opening narration.

7. Name the first episode in which Rod Serling appeared on camera.

8. What series did Rod Serling host after The Twilight Zone?

9. What series did Rod Serling narrate from 1968-1974?

10. What game show did Rod Serling host in 1969?

In This Corner Of The Universe

Name the cities or towns in which the following episodes took place.

1. Walking Distance _____

2. It's A Good Life _____

3. Hocus-Pocus And Frisby _____

4. Nick Of Time _____

5. The Jungle _____

6. Ring-A-Ding Girl _____

7. Mr. Garrity And The Graves _____

8. The Masks _____

9. The Fever _____

10. Stopover In A Quiet Town _____

11. Where does Donlin and his crew crash-land their spaceship?

_____

The Lateness of the Hour
Name the episodes in which the following characters dearly departed.

1. Pinto Sykes _____

2. Rocky Valentine _____

3. Hyder Simpson _____

4. Bartlett Finchley _____

5. Romney Wordsworth _____

6. Erich Streator _____

7. Walter Bedeker_____

8. Nan Adams _____

9. Lew Bookman _____

10. Martin Senescu _____

11. Bunny Blake _____

12. Arch Hammer _____

13. Jason Foster _____

14. Wanda Dunn _____

15. Victoria West _____

16. Paula Dietrich_____

17. Peter Vollmer _____

18. Max Phillips _____

19. Salvadore Ross _____

20. Edward Hall _____

The Three Of Us Are Dying

Match these tragic trios with the episodes they (dis)appeared in.

1. Maj. William Gart, Col. Clegg Forbes and Col. Ed Harrington

2. Capt. Paul Ross, Lt. Ed Mason and Lt. Mike Carter

3. Sgt. William Conners, Pfc. Michael McClusky and Cpl. Richard Langsford

4. James Webber, Kurt Meyers and Peter Kirby

    a. *The 7th Is Made Up Of Phantoms*

    b. *Elegy*

    c. *And When The Sky Was Opened*

    d. *Death Ship*

TZ Fact:

Did you know that Ed Wynn not only starred in two Twilight Zone episodes but he is also mentioned by name in a third? (Static)

Once Upon A Time

Match up the character on the left with his youthful counterpart on the right

Dearly Beloved

Here's your chance to play matchmaker. Simply match up the character on the left with his ever-lovin' on the right.

1.	Hyder Simpson	a.	Annabelle
2.	Henry Bemis	b.	Eileen
3.	Walter Jameson	c.	Helen
4.	Eric Streator	d.	Ellwyn
5.	Allan Ransome	e.	Emily
6.	Walter Bedeker	f.	Laura
7.	Billy-Ben Turner	g.	Laurette
8.	Chester Dietrich	h.	Rachel
9.	Wilfred Harper	i.	Paula
10.	Booth Templeton	j.	Ethel

The Time Element

Name the episodes in which the following characters traveled through time to enter The Twilight Zone.

1. Peter Corrigan _____

2. Martin Sloan _____

3. William Terrance Decker _____

4. Charles Whitley _____

5. Christian Horn _____

6. Gart Williams _____

7. Ed Lindsey _____

8. Paul Driscoll _____

9. Woodrow Mulligan _____

10. Joe Caswell _____

"Look For It Under 'B' For Baseball"

Step up to the plate to answer these national pastime puzzlers.

1. What did Martin Sloan receive on his eleventh birthday?

2. What does Old Ben do when it's his turn to bat?

3. In *What You Need*, Pedott gives Lefty a bus ticket. What is its' destination?

4. In *The Mighty Casey*, what is the first thing that happens to Casey as he steps into the dugout

5. How many games out of first place were the Hoboken Zephyrs before Casey worked his magic?

6. Which of the following ballplayers were never mentioned in a Twilight Zone episode:
    a) Ted Williams
    b) Bob Feller
    c) Joe Dimaggio
    d) Leo Durocher
    e) Mickey Mantle
    f) Willie Mays
    g) Clem Lebine
    h) Robin Roberts
    i) Gil Hodges

7. What other race of "people" had a form of baseball?

8. Why does Captain Benteen put an end to the baseball game in On Thursday We Leave for Home?

The After Hours

Can you help Marsha White find her true identity? Answer the clues below.

E	L	B	M	I	H	T	T	H	E	P	P	I	M
M	R	S	A	R	L	A	T	E	G	A	H	S	A
I	O	T	M	A	R	L	N	N	Q	D	I	I	N
N	O	A	N	B	D	L	I	L	I	E	O	C	N
L	L	Y	A	A	A	L	S	O	H	H	U	N	N
E	F	L	O	F	R	F	O	P	T	C	R	A	O
R	H	O	L	E	O	M	P	G	T	T	S	R	O
L	T	O	S	S	A	D	B	L	H	A	S	F	L
P	N	P	M	O	T	H	E	R	G	R	H	E	F
L	I	L	Z	E	E	H	T	A	U	C	S	N	S
G	N	M	O	A	Z	E	T	Z	G	S	Q	N	I
O	T	R	N	T	T	I	U	Q	S	M	T	A	N
L	S	N	I	U	Q	E	N	N	A	M	U	E	A
E	T	H	T	N	O	M	E	N	O	Y	O	U	R
R	O	O	L	F	D	R	I	H	T	F	O	R	B

1. He managed the department store.

2. What Marsha was shopping for.

3. What it was made of.

4. Who was the gift for?

5. Where the gift was located.

6. What was wrong with the gift?

7. Where you can file complaints.

8. He tried to convince Marsha that there was no ninth floor.

9. The duration of her visit among the "outsiders"

10. He wrote this classic episode.

11. She was Jess-Belle too.

12. What Marsha really was.

Who, What, When, Where
Ten more from . . . The Twilight Zone

1.   I played a nurse and a stewardess in one episode. Who am I ?

2.   I once told a guy 'It has been decided in your favor' and he believed me. What am I?

3.   I never liked actors in undershirts, rock and roll, or Marty Sol for that matter. Who am I?

4.   I just knew I'd be the happiest man on Earth being Leila's lover-marshmallow – but I wasn't. Who am I?

5.   I might give a little. I might take a little. I might even beckon you by name – but I would never deliberately break down. What am I?

6.   If my engines sound desperate, searching it's only because I'm lost and probably low on fuel. What am I?

7.   Soft blouse, flowing skirt, old-fashioned broach and masses of blonde hair. Who am I?

8.   Corwin's cronies come to croon here with Sister Florence. Where am I?

9.   I was gift from that flyspeck next to the river. What am I?

10. I like bowling, potato pancakes and I was a smash on my first day at work. Who am I?

I Got That Kinda Face . . .

Which one of these characters said, "We've gotta infulate 'em to beat the band."?

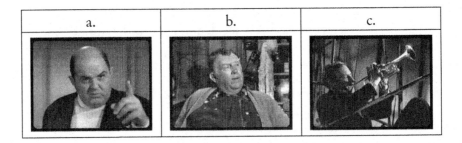

Which one of these characters is really dead?

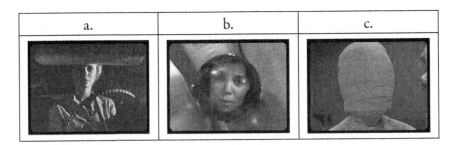

Which one of these characters is on his way to Heaven?

Requiem For A Heavyweight

Step into the ring with these seven knockout questions.

1. In what episode can you find boxer Andy Marshak?

2. What is the name of Bolie Jackson's opponent in The Big Tall Wish?

3. In Steel, what is the classification of the android boxer Battling Maxo?

4. What is the classification of his opponent The Maynard Flash?

5. Which of the following boxers broke his hand before the scheduled fight?

    a) Steel Kelly
    b) Joey Consiglio
    c) Bolie Jackson
    d) Andy Marshak

6. Which of the following episodes took place in Maynard, Kansas?

    a) *The BigTall Wish*
    b) *Requiem For A Heavyweight*
    c) *Steel*
    d) *The Four Of Us Are Dying*

7. How many rounds is Bolie Jackson's fight scheduled for?

The Bard
Match these Twilight Zone writers with the episodes they penned.

Rod Serling

a. The Hunt
Jess Belle
Ring-A-Ding Girl

Richard Matheson

b. Walking Distance
The Eye Of The Beholder
Death's Head Revisited

Charles Beaumont

c. The Invaders
Little Girl Lost
Nightmare At 20,000 Ft.

Earl Hamner Jr.

d. Long Live
The Howling Man
Walter Jameson The Jungle

Name-Game Shame
Match these characters with their less-than-impressive nicknames

1. Clod

    a. Henry Corwin

2. Empty-headed ner-do-well

    b. Jamie Tennyson

3. Harpy

    c. Nora Raigan

4. Moth-eaten Robin Hood

    d. Jonathan West

5. What name is used to describe Jackie Rhodes' intended victim?
    a) Creep
    b) Gleep
    c) Sheep

TZ Fact:

Did you know that while in the Army, Rod Serling had a brief boxing career?

His record; 17 wins – 1 loss

From The Zone And Beyond

Name the Twilight Zone episodes in which the following stars appeared and the TV series they would later star in together.

I	
1. Elizabeth Montgomery	
2. Dick York	
3. Agnes Moorehead	
4. David White	
5. Sandra Gould	
TV Series	

II	
1. William Shatner	
2. Leonard Nimoy	
3. George Takei	
4. James Doohan	
TV Series	

III	
1. Buddy Ebsen	
2. Donna Douglas	
3. Nancy Culp	
4. Raymond Bailey	
TV Series	

Kids Say The Darn-dest Things

The following quotes are from some of Twilight Zone's more youthful inhabitants – can you name them?

1. "I'm the beautiful stowaway!"

2. "We won't fight or cry or make noise . . . y'all hate each other 'cos ya got us."

3. "Hooray for Peter Pan!"

4. "Tell me about the Earth, Captain."

5. "Lotsa kids carve their name here."

The Chaser (Part III)

1. In what three episodes is Death personified?

2. Where does A Game Of Pool take place?

3. In Two, what movie was playing when the world ended?

4. In The Silence, how much does Archie bet Tennyson that he cannot remain silent for one year?

5. In One More Pallbearer, what are the professions of Radin's three visitors?

6. What is the name of the movie that Mike Ferris begins to watch in Where Is Everybody?

7. In The Long Morrow, how many years does Commander Stansfield travel through space?

8. In Showdown With Rance McGrew, what infamous gunslinger visits Rance on the set?

9. In Five Characters In Search Of An Exit, the characters decide to make a human ladder.   What is the order in which they climb?

10. In Queen Of The Nile, what does Pamela Morris use to steal the youth of her victims?

11. In The Jeopardy Room, what is the object that Vassiloff rigs with a bomb?

12. What planet do Conrad and Marcusson visit in People Are Alike All Over?

13. What planet do Sturka, Riden and their families escape to in Third From The Sun?

14. In The Old Man In The Cave, what does the mob find hidden behind the cave door?

15. In The Bard, whom does Moomer unwittingly call upon to help him with his writing career?

16. Where was Henry Bemis having his lunch when the world was destroyed?

17. What year does the atomic war take place in Elegy?

18. In what two episodes can you find Lee Marvin?

19. In The Shelter, who owned the heavy pipe used to break in the door-way?

20. In The Monsters Are Due On Maple Street, whom does Charlie mis-take as an alien and kill?

TZ Speak:

"Even though CBS changed the ending a few times, the comfortable feeling we had was that we rehearsed for two or three days and shot in sequence as a stage production. It was great fun – my son even found an old camera almost exactly like the one we used and I've kept it."

. . . Jean Carson (*A Most Unusual Camera*)

The Parallel

Match the Objects on the left with their rightful owners.

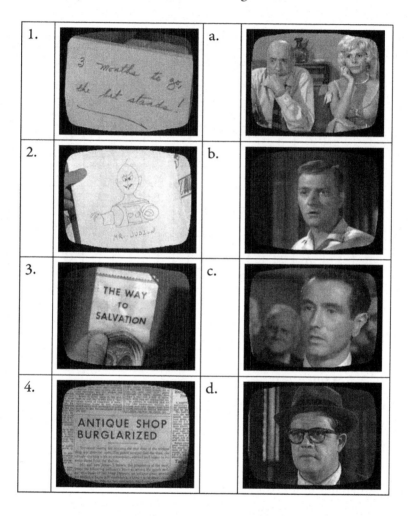

Vera, Vera – Mirror, Mirror

Help Millicent Barnes escape from the Bus Depot by solving the clues below.

M	I	L	E	Z	O	N	A	T	Z	M	C	A	R
C	A	L	H	E	R	S	E	L	F	I	I	L	O
C	U	R	C	I	H	J	U	I	S	S	U	Q	D
R	O	S	T	M	I	L	S	B	E	O	J	U	A
S	E	R	Z	I	Y	Y	L	L	U	T	U	I	E
E	A	V	T	A	N	T	I	L	T	R	I	L	T
G	W	L	T	L	O	M	O	M	V	R	C	O	S
A	O	I	T	B	A	L	I	I	T	I	E	A	N
G	C	G	T	R	L	N	E	L	L	M	J	I	I
G	G	H	E	H	O	L	D	L	N	U	D	G	R
Y	A	V	A	M	J	C	T	I	L	E	Q	H	G
S	B	T	S	A	F	U	Z	O	T	A	R	T	L
P	G	A	R	T	U	C	I	A	R	F	R	L	U
E	S	A	C	F	E	I	R	B	U	A	L	A	A
S	I	S	H	E	R	S	E	L	F	S	O	P	P

1. She was Millicent Barnes.
2. Hers had a broken handle.
3. Where the bus was suppose to take her.
4. He tried to help.
5. What she sees in the mirror.
6. "When not in use, turn off the _____."
7. Who she sees on the bus.
8. He was Paul Grinstead.
9. Where Grinstead's friend lives.
10. "_____ planes."
11. Grinstead lost his.

Deviation From The Norm

Match these less-than-normal characters with the episodes they appeared in.

1.	Goofy Goggles	a. *To Serve Man*
2.	Maya	b. *The Lonely*
3.	Alicia	c. *Steel*
4.	Talky Tina	d. *Perchance To Dream*
5.	Jeremy Wickwire	e. *The After Hours*
6.	The Kanamits	f. *Elegy*
7.	Alan Talbot	g. *Living Doll*
8.	The Gremlin	h. *The Dummy*
9.	Battling Maxo	i. *In His Image*
10.	Marsha White	j. *Nightmare At 20,000 Feet*

You Made Me What I Am Today

Match the actors below with the episodes they appeared in

1.	Earl Holliman	a. *The Last Night of A Jockey*
2.	Mickey Rooney	b. *The Bard*
3.	Robert Duvall	c. *Judgment Night*
4.	Wally Cox	d. *Where Is Everybody?*
5.	James Coburn	e. *Miniature*
6.	Doug McClure	f. *From Agnes – with Love*
7.	James Franciscus	g. *People Are Alike All Over*
8.	Jackie Cooper	h. *Caesar and Me*
9.	Burt Reynolds	i. *Mr. Denton on Doomsday*
10.	Roddy McDowall	J. *The Old Man In the Cave*

A Day At The Races

Win, place or show by matching up the horse with the episode they ran in.

Lane 1: Staunch Soldier   1st Race: *A Most Unusual Camera*

Lane 2: Shady Lane   2nd Race: *A Penny For Your Thoughts*

Lane 3: Tidy Two   3rd Race: *In Praise Of Pip*

Lane 4: Lucky Lady, Crinoline,
         Nimble Runner   4th Race: *What You Need*

Life In The Faust Lane

File these five questions under 'D' for Devil.

1.   In *Printer's Devil* what does "Mr. Smith" do for a living?

2.   What does Walter Bedeker receive in exchange for his soul?

3.   In *The Howling Man*, what does Brother Jerome use to keep the Devil at bay?

4.   What does the Devil call himself in *Escape Clause*?

5.   In *The Chaser*, whom does Roger Shakleforth buy the potions from?

Modus Operandi

Match up the character on the left with the proper Twilight Zone entity.

– Bonus Quiz –

The Chaser (Part IV)

1. In *Jess-Belle*, what does Anne Francis become when midnight strikes?

2. In *The Passersby*, how was Charlie Constable killed?

3. Where does Ace promise to take the cigarette girl?

4. What is the name of the newspaper that Douglas Winter and The Devil work for?

5. In what episode can you visit Cliffordville Indiana in the year 1910?

6. In *Death's Head Revisited*, what do the Dachau inmates sentence Capt. Lutze to?

7. Who portrayed Twilight Zone's first robot?

8. In what episode can you enjoy a cup of Instant Smile?

9. In *You Drive*, what is Oliver Pope guilty of?

10. In *Black Leather Jackets*, what are the names of the three invading aliens?

11. In *A World of Difference*, what two characters are portrayed by Howard Duff?

12. In *Will The Real Martian Please Stand Up?*, what object does Jack Elam salute and request "Take me to your leader."?

13. What is the name of Mr. Bagby's mistress?

14. In what episode can you find Joan Blondell?

15. In *I Am the Night - Color Me Black*, what is the name of the condemned man?

16. In what episode does Ed Wynn play Sam Forstman – lover of clocks?

17. In *Still Valley*, what does Parradine want to use to help end the Civil War?

18. How big does Trooper Franklin estimate the size of the invader in The Fear?

19. In Back There, what is the name of the club that Corrigan belongs to?

20. In *The Little People*, how does Craig communicate with his subjects?

Quick Query

Which of the following episodes does not belong on the list?

a. *Printers Devil,*

b. *Of Late, I Think Of Cliffordville*

c. *Nick Of Time*

d. *Two*

e. *Passage On The Lady Anne*

TZ Fact:

Did you know the educational program 'Cable in the Classroom' uses various *Twilight Zone* episodes to introduce students to concepts such as greed, prejudice, honor and faith?

What's In A (nick) Name?

Match these Twilight Zone characters with the episode that featured
them.

1.	Old Methuselah	a. *The Trouble With Templeton*
2.	Jiggs	b. *Shadow Play*
3.	Fats Brown	c. *The Dummy*
4.	"The Boy Wonder"	d. *A Game Of Pool*
5.	Willy	e. *Ring-A-Ding Girl*
6.	Little Monkey	f. *Person or Persons Unknown*
7.	Powerhouse Baker	g. *The Fugitive*
8.	Kitten	h. *Twenty Two*

9. According to Max Phillips, who is the "queen of women"?

10. What was Henry Francis Valentine better known as?

Please Stand Up!

Help the state troopers solve the mystery of the seventh passenger. Here are the clues.

A	B	O	S	H	K	Q	T	O	A	R	M	S	L
S	D	R	O	M	S	U	N	K	J	I	R	M	H
X	N	I	I	O	L	R	C	J	S	E	L	W	V
O	P	G	R	D	O	L	U	G	P	I	D	K	H
B	O	Q	O	P	G	N	F	O	E	H	A	J	J
E	D	U	E	B	O	E	O	L	F	Y	B	M	I
K	W	I	J	W	B	R	L	O	G	B	R	O	X
U	S	E	N	Q	T	G	E	B	K	L	E	O	E
J	N	I	P	E	O	M	L	V	O	T	C	K	S
E	A	I	T	S	R	J	K	A	I	E	N	X	I
D	G	A	L	I	A	C	B	S	K	R	A	F	N
T	T	H	G	X	B	C	E	S	U	T	D	P	N
S	N	F	Y	B	D	Y	O	U	O	X	O	S	T
A	F	H	E	C	E	O	B	O	X	N	O	G	U
M	A	R	T	I	A	N	L	K	O	Z	E	L	O

1. They followed the aliens' tracks in the snow.
2. Where the tracks led them.
3. He brought the passengers to the diner.
4. She was a professional _____.
5. It played records all by itself.
6. Flying saucer (abbr.)
7. It collapsed under the weight of the bus.
8. *Will The Real _____ Please Stand Up?*
9. The first alien had three of these.
10. The planet from which the counterman came from.
11. The second alien had three of these.

(One) Last Flight

Match the aircraft listed below with the episode that featured them.

1. X-20   a. *I Shot An Arrow In The Air*
2. Arrow 1   b. *On Thursday We Leave for Home*
3. E-89   c. *The Invaders*
4. Pilgrim 1   d. *And When the Sky Was Opened*
5. Probe 1   e. *Death Ship*

Sans Eloquence

Which of the following was not used to describe Twilight Zone dialogue?

1. gibberish

2. Palaver

3. in-again-out-again-Finnigan

4. sentimental hogwash

5. nonsensical doggerel

6. Kentucky windage

Alphabet – Zoup

Name the episode in which episode can Rod Serling be heard saying:

1. "H for haunting"
   a. *The Fugitive*
   b. *The Thirty Fathom Grave*
   c. *What's In The Box?*

2. "B for baseball"
   a. *The Mighty Casey*
   b. *Walking Distance*
   c. *Hocus-Pocus and Frisby*

3. "M for machines"
   a. *Lateness of the Hour*
   b. *A Thing About Machines*
   c. *The Brain Center At Whipple's*

4. "M for mankind"
   a. *The Obsolete Man*
   b. *The Eye Of The Beholder*
   c. *Steel*

5. "G for ghost"
   a. *Night Call*
   b. *The 7th Is Made Up Of Phantoms*
   c. *The Grave*

6. "F for fanatic"
   a. *Person Or Persons Unknown*
   b. *Four O Clock*
   c. *The Old Man In The Cave*

7. "J for justice"
   a. *Four O Clock*
   b. *Dust*
   c. *Escape Clause*

8. "P for phantom"
   a. *The Invaders*
   b. *He's Alive*
   c. *The 7th Is Made Up Of Phantoms*

One Less Pallbearer

Which of the following groups are not made up of phantoms?

The Mirror

Name the characters whose likeness is seen in the mirrors below.

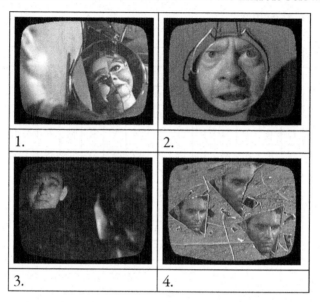

The Eye Of The Beholder

Can you help unravel the bandages that cover Janet Tyler's face? Here are the clues:

C	O	N	F	O	R	M	I	T	Y	E	L	O	P	X	I	N	D	E
E	Y	B	E	H	T	X	Z	A	G	F	T	H	E	E	Y	C	L	D
M	P	T	G	D	A	L	L	A	W	E	R	N	O	S	A	E	R	T
A	O	T	H	E	B	L	D	D	E	L	K	D	R	V	A	A	O	E
X	L	E	G	E	A	N	E	O	F	Z	Y	R	M	E	K	P	W	M
E	R	B	H	R	A	M	L	O	N	O	T	B	T	N	I	S	I	A
S	F	E	E	B	E	A	L	G	D	N	U	R	T	L	N	H	D	E
K	H	A	T	G	Y	X	I	W	L	S	A	E	H	E	T	A	E	R
A	Y	D	J	E	P	Z	H	R	I	U	E	D	R	D	O	D	C	G
E	C	E	O	S	R	O	I	A	T	S	B	R	O	E	O	F	O	N
R	B	A	M	G	E	N	L	S	Y	E	S	N	E	U	N	A	O	I
F	S	R	P	N	T	I	E	P	H	C	A	E	E	R	G	C	P	L
I	O	H	I	I	Y	N	L	L	J	N	S	A	N	S	I	L	L	R
N	T	N	L	P	I	T	B	P	E	D	O	R	O	K	G	E	A	E
O	L	M	S	X	T	W	I	G	Z	V	N	D	S	P	R	H	N	S
L	D	I	A	E	Y	I	G	H	O	S	E	I	E	E	H	A	E	C
M	I	M	L	E	S	E	R	B	A	L	A	N	C	E	T	I	D	S

"A Private ___(1)___ of ___(2)___"

3. Maximum number of experiments

4. It covered her face

5. "A ghetto designed for _____!"

6. "Doctor, you're talking _____!"

7. "This case has upset your _____!"

8. "Glorious _____"

9. "Conform to the _____!"

10. It's in the eye of the beholder

11. Actress under wraps

12. Actress exposed

13. He wrote the episode

TZ Fact:

Did you know that there are efforts underway to develop and issue the first U.S. postage stamp honoring Rod Serling?

More Blankety – Blank Questions

Fill in the blanks to complete the dialogue from various episodes.

1. "I'll say this, your guy knows _____."

2. "Scared old man who don't remember nothing except how to _____."

3. "Watch out for that _____, watch out for that femme fatale."

4. "That's all right operator, I have _____ them."

5. "When you're dead and buried who do you get to _____ for ya?"

6. "I'm just an old fashioned GP, but _____ himself would have something to gnaw on here."

7. "I'll announce when the new_____ will begin."

8. "One drink, one _____ of gold."

9. "I could eat the _____ off a bear. I'm real hungry!"

10. "The eyes lighting up . . . that's the _____ part!"

Walking Distance

Help Martin Find his way home by solving the riddles below.

D	N	O	S	L	I	W	R	M	O	N	K	W	O	N	K	L	S	P
A	A	E	B	E	N	I	U	J	J	S	E	I	K	O	A	U	Q	O
H	E	M	O	M	I	G	D	E	K	O	O	L	X	P	M	D	U	L
S	L	I	R	O	R	G	T	G	J	E	B	D	O	M	G	D	I	H
A	E	C	P	R	O	N	Y	G	H	A	M	O	E	I	G	C	P	Y
L	I	R	Y	I	M	Q	D	H	O	T	R	R	S	I	I	H	O	H
F	M	E	V	N	U	P	R	O	M	T	A	N	Y	N	E	O	O	O
Y	T	S	R	I	O	O	E	M	E	L	H	N	Y	E	Z	C	K	M
E	S	O	E	G	C	S	G	E	W	Q	T	A	B	V	C	O	L	M
P	I	T	R	G	S	E	L	R	O	U	I	C	B	E	L	L	I	O
T	D	L	O	L	L	A	L	R	O	I	G	F	O	L	E	A	W	N
H	R	S	S	B	D	B	A	N	D	C	O	N	C	E	R	T	S	P
A	A	J	M	G	R	B	I	Y	Z	K	W	F	U	O	I	E	O	L
N	M	U	U	I	O	T	B	G	L	N	E	A	B	O	Z	C	N	P
A	R	G	Q	J	R	C	O	R	I	O	V	R	E	O	Y	I	R	M
W	A	L	T	A	L	E	L	O	W	A	I	Y	R	O	H	G	B	I
N	M	O	M	I	M	H	G	D	T	Z	R	D	T	K	C	U	I	L
M	A	R	S	E	S	N	E	C	I	L	S	R	E	V	I	R	D	G

1. "How about some _____"

2. "How about some _____."

3. The town up ahead

4. What the soda was made from

5. He slept in a big, comfortable chair

6. Merry-go-rounds, cotton candy, _____.

7. He was _____ years old when he carved his name on the band-
    stand.

8. "That's the way I _____."

9. "Mom, don't you ____ me?"

10. It expires in 1961

11. It's got a _____ seat

12. "It's _____ I've got to talk to."

13. What they got from the merry-go-round.

14. He was Martin Sloan.

15. "Only one _____ to a customer."

What's In The Box?

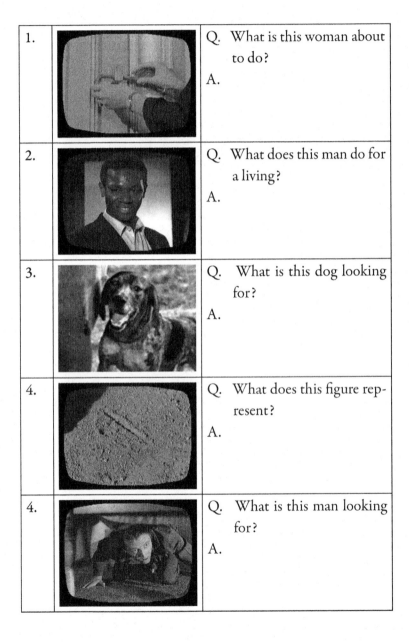

| 1. | | Q. | What is this woman about to do? |
| | | A. | |

| 2. | | Q. | What does this man do for a living? |
| | | A. | |

| 3. | | Q. | What is this dog looking for? |
| | | A. | |

| 4. | | Q. | What does this figure represent? |
| | | A. | |

| 4. | | Q. | What is this man looking for? |
| | | A. | |

– Bonus Quiz –

The Chaser (Part V)
Let's play 20 questions Twilight Zone style!

1. In what episode is Janie Reardon remembered?

2. In *Changing of the Guard*, what state is the Rock Spring School for Boys located?

3. What is Steve, Scott and Fred's favorite form of transportation?

4. In *Nick of Time*, what is it that Don Carter needs to repair his car?

5. In *Night of The Meek*, what song is Sister Florence singing when Santa enters the room?

6. In what episode does Lightning Peterson rise from the dead?

7. What is the name of the man waiting to take Janet Tyler to her new home?

8. In *Four O' Clock*, what sentence does Crangle scribble out of The Gettysburg Address?

9. In *Once Upon A Time*, what is the duration of time travel provided by the helmet?

10. In *Ring-A-Ding Girl*, where was the Founder's Day Picnic held?

11. What does Salvadore Ross trade his broken hand for?

12. In *A Nice Place to Visit*, what was the name of Rocky Valentine's juvenile gang?

13. In *The Shelter*, what did the UFOs turn out to be?

14. In *The New Exhibit*, where does Senescu keep his "Murderers Row"?

15. In *The Lonely*, what are Alicia and Corry doing when they see Allenby's ship?

16. What two restaurants does Gart Williams think Jake Ross might be having lunch?

17. In *Walking Distance*, what is the name of the boy that Martin helps down from the tree?

18. In *From Agnes - with Love*, who does James Elwood have his eye on?

19. In *Passage On The Lady Anne*, who sold the tickets to the Ransome's?

20. Where did Capt. Lutze claim he spent the war years?

TZ Speak:

"Oliver Crangle holds an honored place in my memories. Even my sons, when they were very young, named a couple of items in the house "Oliver" and "Crangle" – and they are so known to this day."

Theodore Bikel (*Four 'O Clock*)

SECTION III:

Master Level of Twilight Zone Knowledge

Filled with any number of rousing riddles, mind-boggling mysteries and crazy contemplations, this final section will truly test your Twilight Zone knowledge.

Submitted for your enjoyment . . .

Master Level of Twilight Zone Knowledge

File It Under 'M' For Music

Answer these musical questions recorded in The Twilight Zone.

In *A Stop at Willoughby*, what song accompanies Gart Williams into the town of Willoughby?

In *Static*, what song does Ed Lindsey hear when he tunes into the past?

In *Mr. Denton on Doomsday*, what song must Al Denton sing in order to get a drink?

In *The Four of Us Are Dying*, what song does Beverly Garland sing?

What song does James Gregory sing in *The Passersby*?

In *Young Man's Fancy*, what is Henrietta Walker's favorite song?

What piece of music does Marge Moore dance to in *A Piano in the House*?

In what episode can you hear Pat Riley play *Moonglow*?

What nursery rhyme does Markie sing in *Nightmare As A Child*?

In what episode can you hear "A Livin' Man"?

Déjá-'View'
Solve these repeating riddles found only in . . . The Twilight Zone:

1. What do Bartlett Finchley and Jana Loren have in common?

2. In what two episodes can you find actor Malcolm Atterbury portraying a traveling salesman peddling his wares from a wagon in the 1880's?

3. Which actor appears 7 times in various episodes and roles?

4. Besides being alone, what do Bemis and McNulty have in common?

5. What two episodes feature the leading man being reduced to ashes?

6. What is unique about Jack Warden's co-stars?

7. *Back There* and *Execution*, what is the central theme and what actor appears in both?

8. What do Anne Henderson and Miss Scott do exactly alike?

9. What do *Judgment Night* and *Shadow Play* have in common?

10. Name the police officer that patrols the streets in *Passage for Trumpet* and *Night of the Meek*

11. In what two episodes can you find a Sheriff Koch?

12. Name three episodes in which the dearly departed use the telephone to communicate with their loved ones.

13. What two episodes take place in a single room and feature the protagonist at war with a mirror?

14. What do *A World of His Own*, *The Fugitive* and *The Obsolete Man* have in common?

15. What two episodes feature characters with a talent for making ships in pictures move?

TZ Speak

"I so admired Rod Serling, and both George Grizzard and Don Gordon are very special actors."

. . . Gail Kobe (*A World of Difference, In His Image* and *Self Improvement of Salvador Ross*)

To Serve Man

Sample today's special from a little cafe just this side of The Twilight Zone

1. What is the name of Don and Pat Carter's lunchtime hangout?

2. How does Jeff Myrtlebank's diet change after he crashes his own funeral?

3. What does Mr. Bevis get from Tony the street vendor?

4. Name the cafe in *Will The Real Martian Please Stand Up*?

5. In *Where Is Everybody?* how does Earl Holliman like his eggs cooked?

6. How does Joe Britt refer to his dinner?

7. In *Shadow Play*, what does Grant do with the D.A.'s T-bone steaks?

8. Where do Jimbo, Ace and Kitty work?

9. In *The Trouble with Templeton* what does Laura enjoy for dinner?

10. What does Mike Ferris help himself to at the drug store?

11. How many eggs does Agnes Grep use to make potato pancakes?

12. In what episode can you get a glass of water at Joe's Airflite Cafe?

13. In what episode can you enjoy some of Mother Connelly's hand-fried eggs?

14. What does Dorn make for Redfield in order to demonstrate Peaceful Valley's atom-assembling device?

15. In *Two*, what type of food do the survivors fight over?

Death Ship

Locate the lost crewmembers of these ill-fated flights of fantasy. (16 possible)

P	I	D	N	O	S	S	U	C	R	A	M	A	G	R	O	P
Z	H	A	P	L	R	E	V	R	A	F	L	A	N	S	E	R
E	O	A	D	I	A	D	E	K	A	L	B	O	T	G	B	D
N	M	A	R	Q	W	I	A	S	E	Y	T	B	K	I	D	E
I	F	B	K	R	U	T	D	N	N	K	S	C	H	A	L	C
M	A	T	R	Y	I	A	J	I	C	S	T	O	S	R	E	K
I	S	T	I	Y	B	N	A	P	O	N	E	E	G	C	I	E
J	A	R	S	L	O	R	G	R	Z	A	B	R	I	K	F	R
L	C	A	N	D	C	O	H	T	Z	R	O	S	L	R	S	W
O	G	G	A	S	R	E	N	N	O	C	L	I	S	A	N	I
D	I	M	B	M	M	A	B	F	A	N	N	Q	U	H	A	O
O	A	K	M	N	E	N	O	Z	C	E	J	I	M	I	T	N
R	D	A	C	O	N	R	A	D	F	S	E	B	N	A	S	P

1. *The Odyssey of Flight 33*   (captain & co-pilot)

2. *King Nine Will Not Return*   (entire crew of 6)

3. *And When The Sky Was Opened*   (3 astronauts)

4. *The Last Flight*   (pilot from 56th squadron RFC)

5. *Judgment Night*   (the U-boat commander)

6. *People Are Alike All Over*   (two astronauts)

7. *The Long Morrow*   (one astronaut)

How's That?

Match the character with the quote.

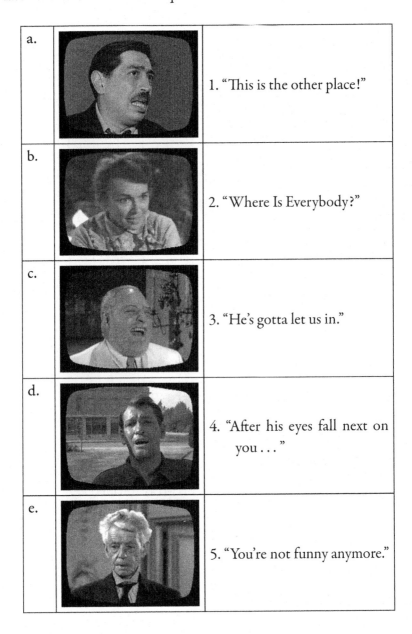

a.		1. "This is the other place!"
b.		2. "Where Is Everybody?"
c.		3. "He's gotta let us in."
d.		4. "After his eyes fall next on you . . ."
e.		5. "You're not funny anymore."

A Penny for Your Thoughts

Can you cash in on these Twilight Zone transactions?

1. How much does Marsha White pay for the gold thimble?

2. How much did Fats Brown's pool cue cost?

3. How much does it cost Philip Redfield to gas up in *Valley of The Shadow*?

    a) $5.00
    b) $5.52
    c) $4.18
    d) $4.42

4. How much does Gallegos pay for the magic dust"?

5. Santa Claus has 6 drinks and a sandwich at Jack's Place. How much does it cost?

    a) $2.75
    b) $3.80
    c) $2.50
    d) $1.61

6. How much does Ed Lindsey have to pay the junk dealer to get his radio back?

7. How much are the Ransome's offered to leave the Lady Anne?

    a) $5,000
    b) $7,500
    c) $10,000
    d) $100,000

8. How much money does Joey Crown pawn his trumpet for?

9. After a visit from the IRS, how much money do the Castle's have left from their million?
   a) $5.00
   b) $1.00
   c) 1 dime
   d) 2 cents

10. How much money does Mike Ferris have in his jumpsuit?

11. How much does Harvey Hunnicut pay for the haunted Model A?

12. In *Nick of Time* how much do Don and Pat Carter's stale sandwiches cost?
    a) $1.80
    b) $2.00 even
    c) $1.50 with 3 cents tax
    d) $1.60 with 3 cents tax

13. How much does it cost Don Carter to call his office

14. How much does the chili cost at the Hi-Way Cafe?
    a) $1.10
    b) $.90
    c) $.95
    d) $1.14 with tax

15. How much does it cost Joe Britt to get his TV repaired?

16. In *Miniature*, how much does Harriet pay for her new dress?

17. In *Will The Real Martian Please Stand Up?*, how much does the Martian's 14 cups of coffee cost him?

18. In *The Jungle*, how much does Alan Richards offer the bum to walk him home?

19. How much does Buster Keaton have to pay for sirloin steak in 1890?

20. How much is Jake Ross's automobile account worth?

21. How much does Fenton agree to pay Arthur (Taro) to care for his lawn each month?

22. In *I Dream of Genie*, how much does George P. Hanley pay for the lamp?

23. In *Steel*, how much does the Battling Maxo team get for their fight with the Maynard Flash?

24. In *Time Enough At Last*, how much does Bemis short-change Mrs. Chester?

25. How much money does Martin Sloan give the counterman for the chocolate ice cream soda?

TZ Speak

"As you know, I did two Twilight Zones (episodes)
and I am very proud of them both"

... Ivan Dixon (*The Bill Tall Wish,*
I Am The Night – Color Me Black)

The Doctor Is In

Can you fill the following prescriptions?

1. In Ring-a-Ding Girl, what does Dr. Floyd "prescribe" for Bunny Blake?

2. Who treated Dave Gurney for his behavioral disorder?

3. How many cases of Epso-Suspendo-Animation have been recorded in 1500 years?

4. Name the doctor who helped save Billy Bayles in Long Distance Call.

5. What time does Janet Tyler receive her sleeping medicine?

6. In The Gift, what does the gift turn out to be?

7. Name the doctor who celebrated a birthday in The Shelter.

8. What did Dr. Loren surround himself with?

9. In King Nine Will Not Return, what does the nurse find in Embry's shoe?

10. In Mr. Denton on Doomsday, what does the doctor declare after examining the gunfighter's hands?

11. In The Mighty Casey, what can't the doctor find when he examines Casey?

12. In What's In The Box, what does the doctor prescribe for Joe Britt?

13. In Last Rites Of Jeff Myrtlebank, what did the doctor do to verify that Jeff Myrtlebank was dead?

14. In Twenty-Two, what is Miss Jameson's duty?

15. Name the doctor who removed Janet Tyler's bandages.

Room For One More Honey . . .

Match up the characters on the left with the correct address or room number on the right.

1.	Gart, Harrington and Forbes	a. Rm. 304
2.	Mrs. Bronson	b. 22437 Ventner Road
3.	Janet Tyler	c. Rm. 15
4.	Peter Corrigan	d. Rm. 14
5.	Arthur Curtis	e. 11 N. 7th St., Apt. 1214
6.	Walter Bedeker	f. Bennett Ave
7.	Jackie Rhodes	g. Rm. 307
8.	Steve, Charlie and Pete Van Horn	h. #19, 12th St.
9.	Arch Hammer	i. Maple St.
10.	Phil Cline	j. Apt. 5B
11.	Stu Tillman	k. 11575 Amanda Drive
12.	Liz Powell	l. Rm. 305

TZ Fact:

Did you know the Twilight Zone continues to be shown in syndication and is represented in cyberspace by devoted fans and their impressive websites? Check:

www.twilightzonemuseum.com
www.twilightzone.org
www.rodserling.com

The Kevin Bacon (7-degree) Twilight Zone Thread, Part I

Kevin Bacon
Movie?
John Lithgow
Movie?
Actress?
Movie?
Richard Dreyfuss
Movie?
Actor?
Twilight Zone Episode?
Ed Wynn

A Most Unusual Camera

Help our three friends escape their fate by solving the riddles below.

T	W	I	G	H	S	O	I	R	U	C	A	L
O	C	A	H	U	M	A	N	I	T	Y	S	R
G	A	A	B	L	U	P	A	P	A	N	D	O
E	N	Q	M	D	R	A	W	D	O	O	W	N
R	E	U	S	E	T	U	H	I	G	L	W	O
E	J	E	A	G	R	L	T	D	L	R	A	S
T	A	W	A	N	F	A	W	T	F	O	U	R
I	P	E	L	L	T	L	E	I	A	E	H	A
A	H	I	H	I	T	N	O	D	R	M	G	C
W	G	G	P	O	L	U	T	T	E	A	T	N
H	I	L	C	R	O	I	K	O	T	C	O	A
M	A	W	A	L	D	K	L	W	S	V	N	E
P	O	H	S	Y	E	C	O	N	E	A	I	J
A	D	S	T	S	U	M	P	T	H	S	E	S
C	L	W	T	Y	Y	T	A	O	C	R	U	F
H	O	O	D	S	U	R	E	I	U	Q	Q	U
G	I	R	P	G	N	I	L	R	E	S	T	R

1. Mr. Dietrich.

2. Mrs. Dietrich

3. He was serving time for breaking and entering.

4. This item had ten to an owner.

5. "You and your _____ shops"

6. What Paula was wearing in the first picture.

7. "Wait a minute Chet, what about_____?

8. The winning horse.

9. "You and your phony_____"

10. The number of available pictures per owner.

11. The Frenchman's job.

12. The number of bodies in the courtyard.

13. She was a fun girl from Mt. Pilot too.

14. He wrote the episode.

How's That Again?

Match the character with the quote.

f.		6. "Well, that's the way it goes."
g.		7. "Strange delusion . . . hearing people's thoughts."
h.		8. "I'll do a jig for you pappy."
i.		9. "You'll never make the grade at anything by playing it safe."
j.		10. "You got the chronology wrong Frank."

Mirror Image
Match the following characters with the actors who portrayed them.

1.	Romney Wordsworth	a. Buster Keaton
2.	Harold Beldon	b. Larry Blyden
3.	Walter Jameson	c. Jack Carson
4.	Millicent Barnes	d. Vera Miles
5.	Fats Brown	e. Buddy Ebsen
6.	James B.W. Bevis	f. Cliff Robertson
7.	Brother Jerome	g. Ida Lupino
8.	Jimbo Cobb	h. Jonathan Winters
9.	Harvey Hunnicut	i. Carol Burnett
10.	Henry Corwin	j. Orson Bean
11.	Anthony Fremont	k. James Whitmore
12.	Christian Horn	l. Pat Hingle
13.	Archibald Beechcroft	m. John Carradine
14.	Michael Chambers	n. Kevin McCarthy
15.	Ramos Clemente	o. Robert Redford
16.	Woodrow Mulligan	p. Donald Pleasence
17.	Rance McGrew	q. Jack Klugman
18.	Agnes Grep	r. Burgess Meredith

19. Prof. Ellis Fowler	s. Lloyd Bochner
20. Horace Ford	t. Peter Falk
21. William Benteen	u. Art Carney
22. Max Phillips	v. Bill Mumy
23. Barbara Jean Trenton	w. Shelly Berman
24. Steel Kelly	x. Ed Wynn
25. Capt. James Embry	y. Robert Cummings
26. Lew Bookman	z. Lee Marvin

Person Or Persons Unknown

Try these ten teasers on Twilight Zone nicknames.

1. Who was Floyd Burney better known as?

2. In what episode can you find 'Big Phil Nolan'?

3. What second season episode features 'Honest Luther Grimbley'?

4. Who was Bunny Blake better known as?

5. What did ventriloquist Jonathan West name his dummy?

6. Who is 'Old Weird Beard'?

7. In what episode can you find 'Old Ben'?

8. What was Helen Foley's nickname as a child?

9. What first season episode features Robert Warwick as 'Old Leadbottom'?

10. What is the name of James Elwood's lovesick computer?

A Collection Of Question Marks

Resolve the riddles below:

1. It's warm, it's July, it's 1888 . . . where am I?

2. No crew, no passengers, no luggage . . . what am I?

3. I wanted the chair but they gave me life . . . who am I?

4. My license plate is 2D-7876 . . . who am I?

5. I sell homes to aliens, my phone number is 485-412 . . . who am I?

6. I fought in two wars, racked up more scared hours than most rabbits, but I like coffee . . . who am I?

7. You could say I was a blue monkey and I might agree with you . . . who am I?

8. It was once known as Satan's Stage Stop, Dead Man's Junction and Boot Hill Village . . . what is it called now?

9. Annabelle and Christie bought a doll on credit here . . . what store am I?

10. The patients like to set me off late at night so they can play outside . . . what am I?

Technical Data

Battle these baffling behind-the-scenes questions.

1. Who held the title of executive producer for The Twilight Zone?

2. What makeup man was responsible for the third eyes and hideous masks of The Twilight Zone?

3. Which of the following produced three seasons of The Twilight Zone?

   a) Buck Houghton
   b) Bert Granet
   c) William Froug
   d) Herbert Hirschman

4. Name the only person to both star in and direct a Twilight Zone episode.

5. What director of photography won an Emmy for his camera work on The Twilight Zone?

6. What do Douglas Heyes, Buzz Kulik, Jacques Tourneur and Richard Donner have in common?

7. What do Mike Ferris's Oakwood High School and Michael J. Fox's Back To The Future clock tower have in common?

8. In what year did The Twilight Zone premiere?

9. Who supplied The Twilight Zone with most of its special effects?

10. On what TV network did The Twilight Zone originally air?

11. TV Guide voted this episode; " the 25th Most Memorable Moment in TV history . . ."

TZ Fact:
Did you know that Twilight Zone's most prolific director was John Brahm? (12 episodes)

Crazy Quilt Of Imagination
Which of these objects can be seen in "The After Hours"?

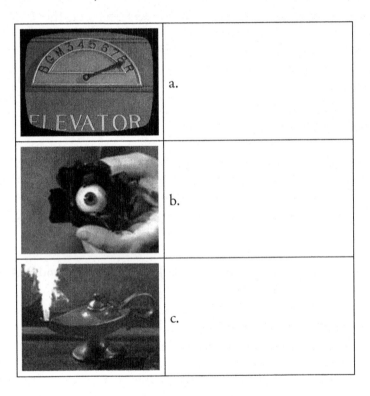

Which of these pictures feature "The Old Man in the Cave"?

d.

e.

f.

Which of these characters is not an alien?

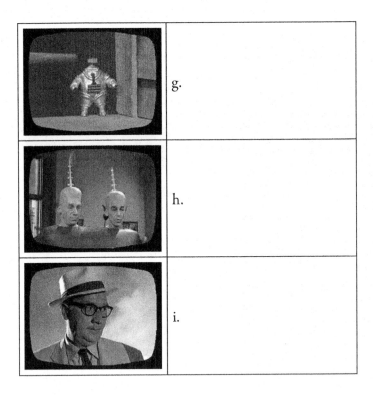

The Four Of Us

Can you stop Arch Hammer before he spreads his reign of terror?
Here are some clues.

G	F	A	K	R	G	I	R	E	T	S	B	O	L	A
I	L	H	M	F	I	A	J	F	E	B	P	Y	C	E
K	M	A	G	A	N	G	S	T	E	R	I	O	I	D
S	J	U	C	B	H	T	N	C	X	E	L	G	I	R
I	G	U	S	S	G	T	E	O	D	A	G	Z	Z	O
H	I	G	D	I	E	F	A	P	A	A	L	Y	O	M
I	Q	U	A	R	C	H	H	A	M	M	E	R	H	A
J	G	D	E	O	A	I	K	P	G	U	N	O	L	R
L	U	X	U	R	O	P	A	X	X	M	R	U	S	S
P	O	A	R	H	F	B	C	N	K	P	A	T	H	H
B	I	S	V	N	H	W	G	W	G	Z	V	N	M	A
O	T	F	M	G	N	I	Y	D	I	H	L	S	T	K
U	P	U	L	S	F	O	S	T	E	R	T	M	U	B

1.   He could make his face change.

2.   He was the first to be impersonated.

3.   Johnny Foster's girlfriend

4.   His profession.

5.   He was the second to be impersonated.

6.   His profession.

7.   He was the third to be impersonated.

8.   His profession.

9.   What his father used to kill him.

10. "...and all four of them were _____"

The Way The Calendar Crumbles

Match the following episodes with the years in which they took place.

1. *The Old Man In The Cave*   a. 1863

2. *The Purple Testament*   b. 1997

3. *Death Ship*   c. 1942

4. *The Passersby*   d. 1890

5. *Mr. Garrity and the Graves*   e. 1865

6. *Judgment Night*   f. 1945

7. *Still Valley*   g. 1974

8. What fifth season episode takes you to the year 2000?

9. In *The Trouble with Templeton*, what year does Booth find himself in when he exits the theater?

10. What second season episode takes place in the years 1847 and 1961?

Flotsam And Jetsam
Which one of these objects was used to contact the dead?

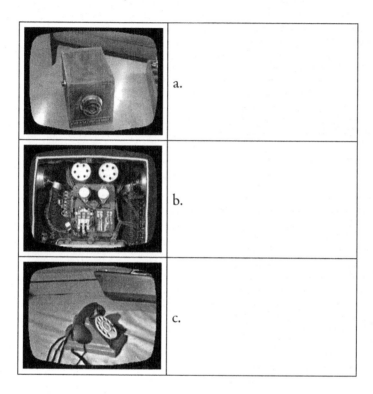

Which one of these objects belongs to Barbara Jean Trenton?

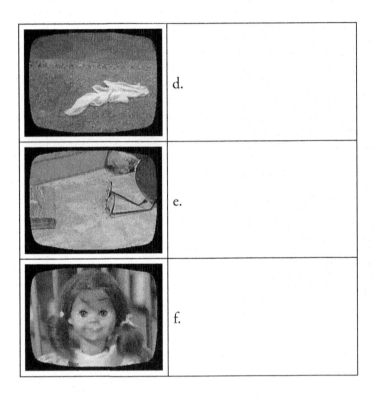

d.

e.

f.

Which one of these objects can give you a fever?

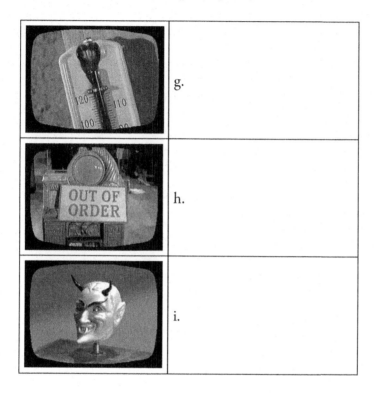

	g.
	h.
	i.

– Bonus Quiz –

The Chaser (Part VI)

1. What character did Gregory West create for *Fury in the Night*?

2. Which of Senescu's wax figures kills his wife?

3. How much can you make for nursing over on the island?

4. What is the population of Peaceful Valley?

5. What does Bob Wilson "drop" in order to obtain the handgun used to eliminate the Gremlin?

6. What is the call sign for Conners, McCluskey and Langsford?

7. What President was assassinated during Paul Driscoll's visit to Homeville?

8. In *Changing of the Guard*, who was the smallest boy to ever play varsity football?

9. What is the population of Cliffordville, Indiana?

10. In *Will The Real Martian Please Stand Up?* what is the call sign for the State Troopers?

11. What year was Grady banned from Hialeah?

12. Where is Mason's Pool Room located?

13. In *On Thursday We Leave For Home*, what is the name of the spacecraft piloted by Col. Sloane?

14. In *A Penny for Your Thoughts*, who was arrested for gambling with company money?

15. In what episode is Fate personified?

16. In what episode can you find Mt. Pilot fun girl Joyce Jameson?

17. What is the name of Jason Foster's doctor?

18. What is the address of Sunnyvale Rest?

19. What is the name of the club that Jonathan West and Caesar burglarize?

20. Why can't Bob Frazier get the car started?

TZ Fact:

Did you know that Liza Minelli once auditioned for but never appeared in a *Twilight Zone* episode?

From The Zone and Beyond . . . Again

Name the Twilight Zone episodes in which you can find these popular personalities.

1. Mayberry RFD's Goober Pyle (George Lindsey).

2. Uncle Charlie (William Demerest) from My Three Sons.

3. Star of Hitchcock's The Birds, (Rod Taylor).

4. Mission: Impossible's Barney Collier (Greg Morris).

5. The bumbling Dr. Smith (Jonathan Harris) from Lost In Space.

6. The Professor (Russell Johnson) from Gilligan's Island.

7. James Bond's merciless enemy "Jaws" (Richard Kiel).

8. Sergeant Carter (Frank Sutton) from Gomer Pyle, U.S.M.C.

9. Sheriff Roscoe P. Coltrane (James Best) from *The Dukes Of Hazzard*.

10. Star Trek's Vulcan ruler (Celia Lovsky)

11. Agent Tom Colby (William Reynolds) from The F.B.I.

12. Hogan Heroes Cpl. Kinchloe (Ivan Dixon).

13. Adm. Harriman Nelson (Richard Basehart) from Voyage To The Bottom Of The Sea.

14. C.O.N.T.R.O.L.'s balding chief (Ed Platt) from Get Smart.

15. Sergeant "Big Toe" Hulka (Warren Oates) from Stripes.

16. S.W.A.T's Lt. Dan Harrelson (Steve Forrest)

17. Scout (Mary Badham) from To Kill A Mockingbird.

18. Tootsie director and co-star (Sydney Pollack).

19. Joan Nash (Patricia Crowley) from Please Don't Eat The Daisies.

20. Batman's Catwoman (Julie Newmar).

21. Mary Tyler Moore Show's Ted Baxter (Ted Knight).

22. Daphne, one of The Andy Griffith Show's Fun Girls from Mt. Pilot (Jean Carson)

23. Bunny Harper (Barbara Stuart) from Gomer Pyle, U.S.M.C.

24. Gomez (John Astin) from The Addams Family.

25. The Avengers' Jonathan Steed (Patrick Macnee).

26. Artemus Gordon (Ross Martin) from The Wild Wild West.

Creature-Feature

Here's ten more to celebrate some of Twilight Zone's lesser-known characters.

1. What three creatures can be seen in *An Occurrence At Owl Creek Bridge*?

2. What were Hyder and Rip in quest of?

3. What is the name of Tina's dog in *Little Girl Lost*?

4. What does Sinclair have on his watch chain?

5. What was Crangle's sidekick?

6. What was George P. Hanley's dog's name in *I Dream of Genie*?

7. What does Gregory West create to keep Victoria from leaving the house?

8. How many heads does Anthony's gofer have?

9. What is the featured television entertainment at Dan Hollis' birthday party?

10. In *The Jungle*, what does Alan Richards find lying outside his apartment

A World Of Possibilities
Complete these multiple-choice queries.

1. What is title of this book? a. The Cure For All Forms of Cancer b. The Private World of Arthur Curtis c. To Serve Man d. None of the Above	
	2. What is the bartender's name? a. Bruce b. Jack c. Beluchi d. Sam
3. Where does this boy send those with bad thoughts? a. Happy Glades b. "secret place" c. The Cornfield d. The Twilight Zone Archives	
	4. Whose coin is this? a. Ace Larsen's b. Franklin Gibbs' c. Hector B. Poole's d. Dave Gurney's

The Kevin Bacon (7-degree) Twilight Zone Thread, Part II

Kevin Bacon
Movie?
Actor?
Movie?
Dan Ackroyd
Movie?
Bill Murray
Movie?
Actor?
Twilight Zone Episode?
Dick York

Cross Over Into . . . The Twilight Zone

Below are the clues, questions and riddles that you'll need to answer in order to complete the crossword puzzle . . .

Across	Down
1. Mr. Smith's favorite waitress	1. Casey's coach
4. Hingle's Horace	2. "_____and shadow"
6. The first thing Renard needed	3. Tennyson's quiet time
9. Mr. Young – (Martin Sloan)	4. Agnes, femme
10. Conrad's sexy Martian	5. Mr. Duryea (Al Denton)
11. Redfield's got him lost	6. Slithers after Finchley
12. What Jameson and Herrick do real fast	7. Powerhouse Baker's first name
13. Franklin's was miserable	8. Hyder's hound
15. He lifted the staff of Truth	14. Crown, Cardiff, Ross and Phillips
20. He was a dead man walking	16. Passage On The _____Anne
22. It landed in Tracy's Pond	17. Makeup Master
23. Elly Glover's horse	18. The Four ___Us Are Dying
25. Rollie was one	19. " He pitches like_____" (two words)
26. They kicked the ____, not the bucket	20. Mr._____ On Doomsday
27. Rooney's jockey	21. "This nightmare begins at _____"
28. Beaumont's killer doll	24. Edward Hall's shrink (initials)
32. Arch was this	29. Nervous Man ___ A Four Dollar Room
33. Adam's pal	30."Mr. Grady, _____ feet tall"
34. Walter's other first name	31. Planet Marcusson died on
35 ._____and Silences	32. Maya ,The _____Girl
37. Renard's leaked	35. The Man
38. The Trouble_____Templeton	36. Science and _____
39. The After _____	37. Cabot's sobriquet
40. He survived Vietnam	38. "____ stinks" (The Purple Testament)
42. Ann Jillian's episode	39. Three season producer
43. Jackie Rhodes' cost four dollars	41. One of five
44. Corrigan's kerchief	42. Klugman's Phillips
47. Not only a tall wish...	44. Lady Anne star (initials)
49. Tennyson's vocal cords	45. On Thursday ___ Leave For Home
51. _____ In The Dark	46. Elva's fiancée
53. Due on Maple ___ (abbr.)	48. ____ A Good Life
54. Marsha, Jess-Belle & Ms. Francis	50. Flora was doing this when Harmon came home.

55. What Mr. Hammer could do with his face	52. Elegy's "Happy" cemetery
58. A vacuum cleaner salesman	56. One bottle left in Peaksville
59. Jimbo's pal	57. What Mr. Chambers was
60. 100 Yards_____ The Rim	58. What Hibbert, Horton, Morgan and Levey do
61. McNulty's waterin' hole	59. Nightmare ___ A Child
62. The Midnight ___	
63. What an edict will not erase	

Cross Over Into . . . The Twilight Zone

ThirtySomething

Match the character on the left with their Twilight Zone age on the right.

1. Arch Hammer   a. 31 years old

2. Sam Conrad

3. Edward Hall   b. 34 years old

4. Fred Renard

5. Martin Sloan   c. 35 years old

6. Warren Marcusson

7. Arthur Curtis   d. 36 years old

8. Ed Harrington

9. Alex Walker   e. 37 years old

10. Gart Williams

11. Jackie Rhodes   f. 38 years old

12. Robert Wilson

13. What age did Pamela Morris claim to be?

All Work And No Play

Punch the clock to answer these hard-working Twilight Zone queries.

1. What does Roswell G. Flemington's company make?

2. How long has Arthur Curtis worked for the Davis-Morton Company?

3. What division does Sturka work for?

4. What kind of project is underway in The Jungle?

5. In Of Late I Think Of Cliffordville, what floor of the Dietrich office building is Miss Devlin's travel service located?

6. In The After Hours, what department does the elevator man claim is on the ninth floor?

7. In The Bard, where does Moomer obtain his black magic research?

8. In I Sing The Body Electric, what magazine features the advertisement for Facsimile Ltd.?

9. In Ring-A-Ding Girl, what was Bud's job at the picnic?

10. In A Piano In The House, where does Fortune buy the piano?

11. Just what does the Cooper Corporation make?

12. Where do Mr. and Mrs. Holt go to buy their new bodies?

13. What does Gart Williams do for a living?

14. In The Encounter, why was Fenton fired from his job?

15. Who offers Barbara Jean Trenton an acting role at International?

16. In The Arrival, whom does Sheckley work for?

17. How long has Dickerson been a foreman at Whipple's?

18. In Young Man's Fancy, what is the name of the Walker's realtor?

19. Besides being a librarian, what other skill did Wordsworth possess?

20. What does Horace Ford do for a living?

TZ Fact:

Did you know that Robert McCord is the only actor to appear in at least one episode from all five seasons of The Twilight Zone?

Read All About It . . .

In what episodes can you read the following headlines?

	1.
THREE SPACEMEN RETURN FROM CRASH; ALL ALIVE	2.
	3.
WORLD WAR II BOMBER FOUND INTACT IN DESERT	4.
H-BOMB CAPABLE OF TOTAL DESTRUCTION	5.
"Our Hero... Woodrow Mulligan... a disgruntled citizen of Harmony, New York ~ 1890"	6.

Quote / unQuote In The Twilight Zone

Name the episodes in which the following lines of dialogue are heard.

1. "Gitchy-gitchy Coo . . . gitchy-gitchy Cooper."

2. "I knowd it! I knowd it! I got a man killed!"

3. "Who ever heard of a dame with a brace being Captain?"

4. "He ain't no student of drama . . . He runs around all the time knockin' Tennessee."

5. "That 'ol woman give us Hail Columbia – stayin' out all night."

6. "Why not a beautiful dame, why not? I never had a dish like that."

7. "Work the gun not the jaws."

8. "My name is Talky Tina and I'm going to kill you."

9. "The rich get richer and the days get shorter."

10. "Radio...it's a world that has to be believed to be seen."

11. "How can you be real when you're made of wood?"

12. "Light in the Salon, let's blackout down there!"

13. " . . . Where your dreams come true after you've stopped dreaming."

14. "To wishes Barbie . . . to the ones that come true."

15. "He's not in his dressing room!"

16. " . . . That's why I made him go on fire."

17. "The first day is the most important date in the life of a play."

18. "You'll never make the grade at anything by playing it safe."

19. "I thought maybe if I could kill him I could make him stop."

20. "The firing squad is for followers not for leaders!"

Twilight Zone Fact Or Fiction (Season One)

Answer these first season true or false queries:

1.	Slippery shoes are the last items given away by Pedott.	T	F
2.	Flora Gibbs first tries her luck on a dollar slot machine.	T	F
3.	Gart Williams' phone number is Capitol-798-99.	T	F
4.	The Glove Cleaner costs $2,500.	T	F
5.	Edward Hall hadn't slept in 87 hours.	T	F
6.	Jerry Hearndan owns a string of supermarkets outside of Chicago.	T	F
7.	Mr. Wirewick is the caretaker of a cemetery in space.	T	F
8.	William Terrence Decker flew in the Royal Air Force.	T	F
9.	Marsha White received a refund for her damaged merchandise.	T	F
10.	Martin Sloan finds a baseball glove in his yard.	T	F
11.	Victoria West was supposed to be at the movies.	T	F
12.	Johnny Foster tells Maggie to run away to New York with him	T	F
13.	Lew Bookman has never been in a helicopter	T	F
14.	Nan Adams uses two twenty dollar bills for the tow and tire change	T	F
15.	Charlie and Liz work Al Denton's favorite saloon	T	F

Twilight Zone Fact or Fiction (Season Two)

Answer these second season true or false queries:

1.	Woodward was serving ten years for breaking and entering.	T	F
2.	John Wilkes Booth's alias was Jonathan Wellington.	T	F
3.	You can get steaks or chops at Freddie Iochino's.	T	F
4.	The Carters order tomato and lettuce on whole wheat.	T	F
5.	Williams is the name of Dr. Loren's handyman.	T	F
6.	The soldier in Two declares peace upon the entire world.	T	F
7.	Santa Claus offers Sister Florence a new hat for Christmas.	T	F
8.	A five-strand hemp rope is used to hang Gallegos.	T	F
9.	King Nine was a B25 Bomber.	T	F
10.	Erbie is the only thief that did not survive suspended animation.	T	F
11.	Counterman Haley hails from Mars.	T	F
12.	Upon removing Miss Tyler's bandage, the doctor says, "Needle, please."	T	F
13.	Billy's late grandmother reads the story of Peter Pan.	T	F
14.	Castle's first wish is to fix the glass in the display case.	T	F
15.	Tennyson's wife loves to shop at Tiffany's	T	F

Twilight Zone Fact or Fiction (Season Three)

Answer these third season true or false queries:

1.	Anthony Freemont hates tomato soup.	T	F
2.	Alex Walker is fond of ice cream cones, the Hardy Boys, and his mom.	T	F
3.	Prof. Fowler has taught at Rock Spring School for Boys for 51 years.	T	F
4.	Jeff Myrtlebank "died" of influenza.	T	F
5.	Georgie owns the club where Jerry and Willy perform.	T	F
6.	Norma paints a waterfall at the behest of Mrs. Bronson.	T	F
7.	Fortune pays $250.00 for the player piano	T	F
8.	Ione takes a dinner plate to Pinto's grave.	T	F
9.	Fats and Joey play several games of 8-ball.	T	F
10.	Charlie runs through the sprinklers at the Shadyvale Rest Home.	T	F
11.	Old Ben changes into a monster, a mouse and a fly.	T	F
12.	Mr. Faraday folds with a winning hand.	T	F
13.	Evil people will be 4feet. tall at 4 o'clock.	T	F
14.	Frisby studied math at the University of Wichita.	T	F
15.	According to Frank, Jerry Etherson ran out on 115 performances	T	F

Twilight Zone Fact or Fiction (Season Four)

Answer these fourth season true or false queries:

1.	Charley Parks gets fired because he just doesn't fit in.	T	F
2.	The Lady Anne belonged to the Royal Star Line.	T	F
3.	Philip Redfield's car is destroyed by a huge rock.	T	F
4.	President Kennedy is mentioned in The Parallel.	T	F
5.	Mr. Smith lights his cigar from a flame that comes from his finger	T	F
6.	Capt. Benteen had to deal with two suns perpetually shining.	T	F
7.	Paul Driscoll escapes to Centerville, Indiana.	T	F
8.	In The Thirty-Fathom Grave the strange sound is coming from a lost galleon.	T	F
9.	Jess-Belle tries to trade a silver hairpin for the love of Billy Ben.	T	F
10.	Hermy Brandt knocks the watch out of Horace Ford's hand.	T	F
11.	Ross, Mason and Carter's mission was to obtain planetary samples.	T	F
12.	Ilse Nielsen deliberately sets the fire that destroys her home.	T	F
13.	Jess-Belle shows up at the wedding as a spider.	T	F
14.	Alan Talbot makes his home in Cottonwood.	T	F
15.	Shannon Foods is sponsoring Moomer's The Tragic Cycle.	T	F

Twilight Zone Fact or Fiction (Season Five)

Answer these fifth season true or false queries:

1.	Aunt T and the kids bake a huge chocolate pie together.	T	F
2.	Freddy Broom is the butcher that's got his eye on Phyllis Britt.	T	F
3.	The Masks takes place during the Mardi Gras.	T	F
4.	Mr. Grady's real name is Michael.	T	F
5.	Elva's fiancé is buried in Valley View Cemetery.	T	F
6.	Mr. Wilson flew on Gold Star Airways.	T	F
7.	Conners, McCluskey and Langsford drove their tank into the battle.	T	F
8.	The first person to appear his Bunny's ring is Cyrus Gentry.	T	F
9.	Vassiloff's hit man's name is Igor.	T	F
10.	Rod Serling scripted 92 of the 156 Twilight Zone episodes.	T	F
11.	Battling Maxo was from Philadelphia.	T	F
12.	Goldsmith's people destroy the "Old Man" with a grenade.	T	F
13.	Oliver Pope's felony takes place at 3rd & Main.	T	F
14.	Harmon Gordon paid $1,000 for the youth serum.	T	F
15.	Jagger is to be hanged at 9:30 in the morning.	T	F

The Little People
Identify these characters featured in supporting roles

	1.
	2.
	3.
	4.
	5.
	6.

The Little People - continued

	7.
	8.
	9.

The Kevin Bacon (7-degree) Twilight Zone Thread, Part III

Kevin Bacon
Movie?
Joe Peschi
Movie?
Actor?
Movie?
Tom Cruise
Movie?
Actor?
Twilight Zone Episode?
William Windom

Made Up Of Phantoms

Name the episodes in which the following characters were mentioned but never seen.

1. Teddy Reynolds
2. Fred Jackson
3. Phillip Waynewright
4. Freddy Broom
5. Dr. Bradbury
6. Guynemer
7. Manolete
8. Steve Black
9. Mickey Spillane
10. Silky Armstrong
11. Curt J. Lucas
12. Bob Blair's wife
13. Perry Como
14. The Ray-Tones
15. Ray Bradbury

What You Need

Match up the faithful servant on the left with the correct episode on the right.

1. Marvin

2. Reynolds

3. Robert

4. Jeffery

5. Margaret

6. Franklin

7. Williams

8. Marty

9. Sally

10. Charlotte

a. *The Trouble with Templeton*

b. *The Silence*

c. *Spur of the Moment*

d. *A Piano in the House*

e. *The Masks*

f. *Queen of the Nile*

g. *Night Call*

h. *The Sixteen-Millimeter Shrine*

i. *Back There*

j. *Lateness of the Hour*

The Invaders

Can you help the woman fend off her alien attackers? Use the clues listed below:

E	E	A	T	W	I	L	H	J	U	Q	U	S	A	S
X	D	E	A	H	M	B	O	N	F	E	E	A	L	T
A	P	O	O	A	L	R	A	O	L	B	L	M	O	N
G	G	H	T	R	A	E	H	S	O	E	E	L	P	A
I	G	N	G	P	L	A	C	E	S	E	A	D	L	I
A	B	K	E	C	Z	D	A	H	K	G	R	O	Y	G
B	G	O	E	S	O	I	R	T	I	S	O	P	T	H
F	N	R	N	F	M	T	S	A	R	T	O	O	Y	T
D	S	L	E	I	N	O	M	M	D	S	B	T	W	Z
I	F	L	O	S	E	K	O	D	G	I	L	Q	I	O
A	X	A	O	N	H	L	W	R	H	M	A	U	L	S
L	Z	E	R	Q	P	A	E	A	E	P	N	O	G	E
O	U	V	F	U	L	A	M	H	O	H	K	P	R	C
G	O	G	N	I	K	O	O	C	S	L	E	O	O	S
U	P	L	R	T	N	C	T	I	T	E	T	A	O	E
E	R	O	R	W	Q	K	S	R	H	S	F	O	D	A
S	D	V	A	I	U	J	P	C	W	O	O	L	N	F
S	E	Y	E	H	S	A	L	G	U	O	D	K	A	K

1. "This is one of the out-of-the-way-_____"

2. What the woman is doing when the aliens land.

3. One of them burns a hole through her_____.

4. One of them is hiding under a _____.

5. One of them cuts her with her own _____.

6. One of them is hiding under the _____.

7. What she uses to destroy the spacecraft.

8. Where the aliens are from.

9. "Incredible race of _____"

10. He died in the attack.

11. She portrayed the woman.

12. This starring role had no _____.

13. He directed the episode.

14. He wrote the episode.

Still More Blankety-Blank Questions

Fill in the blanks to complete the Twilight Zone dialogue.

1. "There are some moments in life that have an indescrib-able_____."

2. "I_____ you're going my way."

3. "I've come too far, too fast to get stuck out here in _____."

4. "_____ demands the theatrical."

5. "How come you're _____ years old again Pip?"

6. "If I had a dime for every time I whopped you, I'd have _____ dollars."

7. "It's not the _____ I'm talking about, it's books and study."

And Now Mr. Serling . . .

Name the episodes that Rod Serling is introducing.

	1.
	2.
	3.
	4.
	5.
	6.

And Now Mr. Serling . . . continued

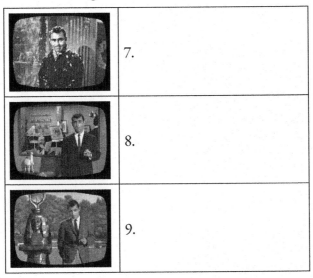

	7.
	8.
	9.

Déjá-'View' All Over Again
More repeating riddles from the Twilight Zone

1. What do Timmy Danvers and Fred Renard have in common?

2. What episode's first act and final act are identical?

3. What three episodes feature a Roll-a-Top one-armed bandit?

4. Name two episodes in which the same actor is shot and killed in the final act.

5. What do Uncle Simon and Markie have in common?

6. What three episodes feature planets or asteroids with two suns?

7. What actor and actress appear together in a first season and a forth season episode?

8. What two episodes feature Forbidden Planet's Robby the Robot?

– Bonus Quiz –

The Chaser VII

1. What type of refreshment does Norma manage to obtain from the supermarket?

2. What third season episode takes place in 1942 and 1945?

3. In what episode do we meet Otto Champion?

4. In what order do the Astronauts disappear in And When the Sky Was Opened?

5. What did Gooberman's wife Zelda weigh at the time of her demise?

6. What is the name of the nightclub in which Caswell destroys the jukebox and TV?

7. What does James Corry make to help pass the time?

8. How many times does Phyllis Britt have to heat up Joe's dinner?

9. In what episode is it a crime to own a Bible?

10. Who performed the task of burying Rip?

11. In The Grave, who did Conny Miller ask to guard the bets?

12. In A Passage for Trumpet, how long had the bus driver gone without an accident?

13. In Judgment Night, what time does Lanser think something is going to happen?

14. What is the name of the museum that Charley frequents in Miniature?

15. In what episode do we find Mayor Finch?

16. How many astronauts are aboard the ill-fated Arrow One?

17. What is the name of the potion that Fate gives Denton and Grant?

18. Where does Woodrow Mulligan take the Time Helmet for repairs?

19. Name the character that traveled 25 years into the past to save herself

20. What does Andy Praskins do for a living?

TZ Speak

"Because we (actors and writers) cared so much about what we were doing then . . . we are immortal now – The Twilight Zone will live forever"

. . . famed Twilight Zone writer, George Clayton Johnson

Congratulations!

With your training now complete and your quest for knowledge fulfilled, you have earned the degree of

Master of Twilight Zone Knowledge

For Starters

1. False
2. True
3. False
4. True
5. True
6. False
7. True
8. True
9. True
10. True

Sounds and Silences

1. Through
2. Dimension
3. Sight
4. Wondrous
5. Boundaries
6. Imagination
7. Signpost
8. Stop

Patterns

1. *Static*
2. *Two*
3. *Dust*
4. *Elegy*
5. *Execution*
6. *Mute*
7. *Steel*

Picture If You Will

D.

Where Is Everybody?

1. *Jameson*
2. Mr. Death
3. *Midnight Sun*
4. Corwin
5. *Odyssey*
6. *Pip*
7. Kanamits
8. *Howling*
9. Homewood
10. *Time*
11. *Shadow*
12. *Willoughby*
13. The Twilight Zone
14. Cornfield
15. Trumpet
16. *Dream*
17. Rod Serling
18. Bemis
19. *After Hours*
20. *Hitchhiker*
21. Crangle
22. *Beholder*
23. *Doomsday*
24. *Bewitchin' Pool*
25. *Dingle*
26. *Invaders*

27. *Templeton*
28. *Doll*
29. Fifth Dimension
30. *Obsolete*

More Sounds And Silences

1. Door
2. Imagination
3. Dimension
4. Sight
5. Sound
6. Mind
7. Land
8. Shadow
9. Ideas
10. Crossed
11. Twilight

Synonymically Speaking

1. g.
2. d.
3. i.
4. b.
5. f.
6. e.
7. a.
8. j.
9. c.
10. h.

A Short Drink

1. d
2. f
3. a
4. g
5. b
6. i
7. e
8. j
9. h
10. c

A Little T Z Q & A

Because he finally gets to read
To undergo an operation to fix
    her hideous face
A third eye
A Gremlin

From Boss To Blockhead

1. c
2. g
3. j
4. b
5. d
6. i
7. e
8. a
9. f
10. h

The Chaser (Part I)

1. The ashtrays were full
2. Charles Bronson and Elizabeth Montgomery
3. The Glove Cleaner
4. Aunt T
5. WPDA
6. *Mr. Dingle, The Strong*
7. *The New Exhibit*
8. *Where Is Everybody?*
9. 20 dollar gold piece
10. The Devil
11. 100 years
12. *Mr. Denton On Doomsday, The Jeopardy Room*
13. A slot machine
14. He walks
15. *Mirror Image*
16. Jerry Herndon
17. Life or death
18. Neighborhood boy played by Ron Howard in *Walking Distance*
19. *It's A Good Life*
20. *Nightmare As A Child, Valley Of The Shadow, Caesar And Me*

Fame And Misfortune

b.

The Thirty Fathom Grave

d.

The Mind and The Matter

1. Stopwatch
2. Camera
3. Shoes
4. Mirror
5. Bottle
6. Can
7. Penny
8. Box

The Silence

c. b

Crime And Comeuppance

1. d
2. a
3. e
4. c
5. b

What's Mine Is Mine

1. i
2. c
3. b
4. g

5. h
6. e
7. a
8. f
9. j
10. d

Still More Sounds and Silences

1. Fifth
2. Known
3. Vast
4. Space
5. Infinity
6. Light
7. Superstition
8. Pit
9. Summit
10. Knowledge
11. Imagination
12. Call
13. Zone

A Thing About Numbers

1. *7th*
2. *One*
3. *Sixteen*
4. *Nine*
5. *33*
6. *Third*
7. *Four*
8. *Four*
9. *Hundred*
10. *Five*
11. *Four*
12. *Thirty*
13. *20,000*
14. *Twelve*
15. *7*
16. *Ninety*

The Chaser (Part II)

1. Penicillin
2. Eleven
3. A harmonica
4. Hell
5. It is the file number of the photo that Dave Gurney believes will assure his sanity and identity
6. 1924 Rickenbacker
7. Iwo Jima
8. Five
9. St. Nicholas Arena (St. Nick's)
10. Agnes Grep
11. *A Game Of Pool, A Penny For Your Thoughts, Kick The Can, Nothing In The Dark*
12. Jack Klugman
13. Guitar
14. *Walking Distance*

15. He throws him over a balcony to fall on the crowd below
16. Fashion Editor
17. Burgess Meredith
18. A new front name
19. She backs off the roof of the apartment building with a little help from Mr. Bedeker
20. "What To Do When Booth Comes Back"

Pleased To Present Mr. Rod Serling

1. b
2. a
3. c
4. b
5. a
6. *Odyssey of Flight 33, An Occurrence at Owl Creek Bridge*
7. *A World Of His Own*
8. Night Gallery
9. The Undersea World of Jacques Cousteau
10. The Liar's Club

In This Corner Of The Universe

1. Homewood

2. Peaksville, Ohio
3. Pitchville Flats
4. Ridgeview, Ohio
5. New York, NY
6. Howardville
7. Happiness, Arizona
8. New Orleans
9. Las Vegas
10. Centerville
11. Reno, Nevada

The Lateness of the Hour

1. *The Grave*
2. *A Nice Place to Visit*
3. *The Hunt*
4. *A Thing About Machines*
5. *The Obsolete Man*
6. *Living Doll*
7. *Escape Clause*
8. *The Hitchhiker*
9. *One For the Angels*
10. *The New Exhibit*
11. *Ring-A-Ding-Girl*
12. *The Four of Us are Dying*
13. *The Masks*
14. *Nothing in the Dark*
15. *A World of His Own*
16. *A Most Unusual Camera*
17. *He's Alive*
18. *In Praise of Pip*

19. *The Self-Improvement of Salvadore Ross*
20. *Perchance to Dream*

The Three of Us Are Dying

1. c
2. d
3. a
4. b

Once Upon A Time

1. e
2. a
3. d
4. b
5. c

Dearly Beloved

1. h
2. c
3. g
4. a
5. b
6. j
7. d
8. i
9. e
10. f

The Time Element

1. *Back There*
2. *Walking Distance*
3. *The Last Flight*
4. *Kick The Can*
5. *A Hundred Yards Over the Rim*
6. *A Stop at Willoughby*
7. *Static*
8. *No Time Like The Past*
9. *Once Upon A Time*
10. *Execution*

Look For It Under 'B' For Baseball

1. A baseball glove and a ball autographed by Lou Gerhig
2. He hits a home run
3. Scranton, PA
4. He gets hit in the head with a foul ball
5. 31 games
6. Mickey Mantle
7. The Kanamits
8. He felt it was too hot

The After Hours

1. Sloan
2. Thimble
3. Gold
4. Mother

5. Ninth Floor
6. Scratched
7. Third Floor
8. Armbruster
9. One Month
10. Serling
11. Anne Francis
12. Mannequin

Who, What, When, Where

1. Arline Sax (Arlene Martel)
2. The Mystic Seer
3. Barbara Jean Trenton
4. Roger Shackleforth
5. Franklin Gibbs' favorite slot machine
6. Flight 33 from London to New York
7. Mary (Gregory West's mistress)
8. Delancy Mission
9. Bunny Blake's ring from her fans in   Howardville
10. Agnes Grep

I Got That Kinda Face

b
a
b

Requiem For A Heavyweight

1. *The Four Of Us Are Dying*
2. Joey Consiglio
3. B2
4. B7
5. c. Bolie Jackson
6. c. *Steel*
7. 10 rounds

The Bard

b

c

d

a

Name-Game Shame

1. d
2. b
3. c
4. a
5. b

From The Zone And Beyond

I

1. *Two*
2. *A Penny For Your Thoughts, The Purple Testament*
3. *The Invaders*
4. *I Sing The Body Electric, A*

World of Difference
5. *What's In The Box,
   Cavender Is Coming
   Bewitched*

II

1. *Nick of Time, Nightmare at
   20,000 Feet*
2. *A Quality of Mercy*
3. *The Encounter*
4. *Valley of the Shadow Star
   Trek*

III

1. *The Prime Mover*
2. *The Eye of the Beholder, Cavender is Coming*
3. *The Fugitive*
4. *Escape Clause, Back There,
   From Agnes - With Love
   The Beverly Hillbillies*

Kids Say The Darn-dest Things

1. Jenny
2. Sport
3. Billy Bayles
4. JoJo
5. Martin Sloan

The Chaser (Part III)

1. *One For The Angels, The
   Hitchhiker, Nothing In The
   Dark*
2. Lister's Pool Room,
   Randolph Street, Chicago
3. Furlough Romance
4. $500.000
5. A General, A Reverend,
   A Teacher
6. Battle Hymn
7. 40
8. Jesse James
9. 1st Major, 2nd Clown, 3rd
   Hobo, 4th Bagpiper, 5th
   Ballet Dancer
10. A rare Egyptian Beetle
11. The telephone
12. Mars
13. The Earth
14. A Computer
15. William Shakespeare
16. The bank vault
17. 1985
18. *The Grave, Steel*
19. Phil Cline
20. Pete Van Horn

The Parallel
1. c
2. d
3. b
4. a

Vera, Vera, - Mirror, Mirror
1. Vera Miles
2. Bag
3. Cortland
4. Paul Grinstead
5. Herself
6. Juice
7. Herself
8. Martin Milner
9. Tully
10. Parallel
11. Briefcase

Deviation From The Norm
1. h
2. d
3. b
4. g
5. f
6. a
7. i
8. j
9. c
10. e

You Made Me What I Am Today
1. d
2. a
3. e
4. f
5. j
6. i
7. c
8. h
9. b
10. g

A Day At The Races
Lane 1 – 4th Race
Lane 2 – 3rd Race
Lane 3 – 1st Race
Lane 4 – 2nd Race

Life In The Faust Lane
1. Linotype Operator/ Reporter
2. Immortality
3. The Staff of Truth
4. Cadwallader
5. A Daemon

Modus Operandi

1. b
2. e
3. a
4. d
5. c

The Chaser (Part IV)

1. A Leopard
2. Shot through the head at Gettysburg
3. Lake Mead
4. Dansburg Courier
5. *Of Late I Think of Cliffordville*
6. Insanity
7. Jean Marsh
8. *Number Twelve Looks Just Like You*
9. Hit and run driving
10. Steve, Scott and Fred
11. Arthur Curtis, Jerry Raigan
12. The Jukebox
13. Felicia
14. *What's In The Box?*
15. Jagger
16. *Ninety Years Without Slumbering*
17. Witchcraft
18. 500 ft. Tall
19. The Potomac Club
20. Mathematics

Quick Query

e. *Two*
The other episodes all feature actors that were guest stars on Batman.

What's In A (nick) Name?

1. e
2. b
3. d
4. a
5. c
6. g
7. f
8. h
9. Mrs. Feeney
10. Rocky Valentine

Please Stand Up!

1. State Troopers
2. Diner
3. Bus Driver
4. Dancer
5. Jukebox
6. UFO
7. Bridge
8. Martian
9. Arms
10. Venus
11. Eyes

(One) Last Flight

1. d
2. a
3. e
4. b
5. c

Sans Eloquence

d.

Alphabet – Zoup

1. b
2. a
3. b
4. a
5. c
6. b
7. a
8. c

One Less Pallbearer

b

The Mirror

1. Willy
2. Grady
3. Mr. Death
4. Lt. Fitzgerald

The Eye Of The Beholder

1. World
2. Darkness
3. Eleven
4. Bandage
5. Freaks
6. Treason
7. Balance
8. Conformity
9. Norm
10. Beauty
11. Maxine Stuart
12. Donna Douglas
13. Serling

More Blankety-Blank Questions

1. Clothes
2. Bleed
3. Female
4. Reached
5. Mourn
6. Freud
7. Day
8. Bar
9. Hide
10. Beauty

Walking Distance

1. Service
2. Quiet
3. Homewood
4. Chocolate
5. Mr. Wilson
6. Band concerts
7. Eleven
8. Looked
9. Know
10. Driver's license
11. Rumble
12. Martin
13. Limp
14. Gig Young
15. Summer

What's In The Box?

1. Set the Devil free
2. Heavyweight Boxer
3. Raccoon or maybe Heaven
4. Telephone poles
5. His daughter

The Chaser (Part V)

1. *Nervous Man In A Four Dollar Room*
2. Vermont
3. Motorcycles
4. Fuel pump
5. Joy To The World

6. *Mr. Garrity and the Graves*
7. Mr. Walter Smith
8. All men are created equal
9. 30 minutes
10. Riverside Park
11. A cold/cough
12. The Angels
13. Satellites
14. In his basement
15. Star gazing
16. Sardi's East, The Colony
17. Bobby
18. Millie
19. Mr. Spireto
20. On The Russian Front

File It Under 'M' For Music

1. 'Beautiful Dreamer'
2. 'I'm Getting Sentimental Over You'
3. 'How Dry I Am'
4. 'One More for the Road'
5. 'Black is the Color of My True Love's Hair'
6. 'The Lady in Red'
7. Clair de Lune
8. *It's a Good Life*
9. 'Twinkle, Twinkle, Little Star'
10. *An Occurrence at Owl Creek Bridge*

Dèjá-View

1. In addition to being surrounded by machines they detest, they both like to stand at the top of the stairs and yell "Machine(s)!"
2. *Mr. Denton On Doomsday, Of Late I Think Of Cliffordville*
3. Jay Overholts
4. They both break their timepieces on the floor of a bank.
5. *Long Live Walter Jameson, Queen of the Nile*
6. They are robots.
7. Time travel, Russell Johnson.
8. Their screams are identical.
9. The protagonist must be condemned over and over again.
10. Officer Flaherty
11. *Dust, I Am the Night-Color Me Black*
12. *The Hitchhiker, Long Distance Call, Night Call*
13. *Nervous Man in a Four Dollar Room, Last Night of a Jockey*
14. Rod Serling appears at the end of each episode.
15. *Perchance To Dream, Mute*

To Serve Man

1. Busy-Bee Cafe
2. He only eats two eggs.
3. An apple
4. Hi-way Cafe
5. Over-easy
6. Tastes like corrugated plastic
7. He turns them into a roast
8. Happy-Daze Cafe
9. Steak (The Kansas City)
10. Ice Cream Sundae
11. An even dozen
12. *A Hundred Yards Over the Rim*
13. *In His Image*
14. Ham Sandwich on white bread with mustard
15. Canned chicken

Death Ship

1. Farver, Craig
2. Embry, Kline, Conners, Cransky, Jimenez, Blake
3. Harrington, Forbes, Gart
4. Decker
5. Lanser

6. Conrad, Marcusson
7. Stansfield

How's That?

a. 3
b. 4
c. 1
d. 2
e. 5

A Penny For Your Thoughts

1. $22.80, ($25.00 with tax)
2. $600.00
3. d. $4.42
4. 100 pesos
5. b. $3.80
6. $10.00
7. $10,000
8. $8.50
9. a. $5.00
10. $2.85
11. $25.00
12. d. $1.60 with 3 cents tax
13. 75 cents
14. b. $.90
15. No charge
16. $20.00
17. $1.40
18. $10.00
19. 17 cents per pound
20. Approximately 3 million dollars
21. $7.00
22. $20.00
23. $250.00
24. $1.00
25. $1.00

The Doctor Is In

1. Rest, sleep, fresh air and some of Hildy's good cooking
2. Dr Koslenko
3. 30
4. R. Unger M.D.
5. 9:30
6. The cure for cancer
7. Dr. Stockton
8. Robots
9. Sand
10. A push – no winner
11. A pulse/heartbeat
12. Tranquilizers
13. He stuck him with a pin
14. Night nurse in charge of the basement floor
15. Dr. Bernardi

Room For One More Honey . . .

1. c
2. j
3. g
4. h
5. b
6. e
7. d
8. i
9. a
10. f
11. k
12. l

Kevin Bacon (7-degree) Twilight Zone Thread Part I

Footloose
Harry And The Hendersons
Melinda Dillon
Close Encounters of the Third Kind
The Graduate/Jaws
Murray Hamilton
One For The Angels

A Most Unusual Camera

1. Chester
2. Paula
3. Woodward
4. Camera
5. Curio
6. Fur Coat
7. Humanity
8. Tidy Two
9. Palpitations
10. Ten
11. Waiter
12. Four
13. Jean Carson
14. Serling

How's That Again?

f. 10
g. 6
h. 9
i. 7
j. 8

Mirror Image

1. r
2. o
3. n
4. d
5. h
6. j
7. m
8. e
9. c
10. u
11. v

12. f
13. w
14. s
15. t
16. a
17. b
18. i
19. p
20. l
21. k
22. q
23. g
24. z
25. y
26. x

Person Or Persons Unknown

1. The Rockabilly Boy
2. *The Prime Mover*
3. *The Whole Truth*
4. The Ring-A-Ding Girl
5. Caesar
6. Prof. Ellis Fowler
7. *The Fugitive*
8. Markie
9. *The Last Flight*
10. Agnes

A Collection Of Question Marks

1. Willoughby
2. Flight 107
3. Walter Bedeker
4. Nan Adams
5. R.C. Jones
6. Trooper Franklin
7. Charley Parkes
8. Happiness, Arizona
9. Mason's
10. Firecrackers

Technical Data

1. Rod Serling
2. William Tuttle
3. a Buck Houghton
4. Ida Lupino
5. George T. Clemens
6. They all directed Twilight Zone episodes
7. They are one in the same – (filmed at Universal Studios)
8. 1959

9. Virgil Beck
10. CBS
11. *Time Enough At Last*

Crazy Quilt Of Imagination

a

e

g

The Four Of Us . . .

1. Arch Hammer
2. Foster
3. Maggie
4. Musician
5. Sterig
6. Gangster
7. Marshak
8. Boxer
9. Gun
10. Dying

The Way The Calendar Crumbles

1. g
2. f
3. b
4. e
5. d
6. c
7. a

8. *Number Twelve Looks Just Like You*
9. 1927
10. *A Hundred Yards Over The Rim*

Flotsam And Jetsam

c.

d.

h.

The Chaser (Pt. VI)

1. Phillip Waynewright
2. Jack The Ripper
3. $15.00
4. 981
5. a pack of cigarettes
6. Bluebird 9
7. Garfield
8. Bill Hood
9. 779
10. 1183A
11. 1961
12. Sandusky, Ohio
13. Galaxy 6
14. Mr. Sykes
15. *Mr. Denton On Doomsday*
16. *I Dream Of Genie*
17. Dr. Thorn
18. 478 Tranquility Lane
19. The Carioca Club
20. There's no engine in it

From The Zone And Beyond . . . Again

1. *I Am The Night-Color Me Black*
2. *What's In The Box*
3. *And When The Sky Was Opened*
4. *The 7th Is Made Up of Phantoms*
5. *The Silence, Twenty Two*
6. *Back There, Execution*
7. *To Serve Man*
8. *The Dummy*
9. *The Grave, Jess-Belle, Last Rites of Jeff Myrtlebank*
10. *Queen of the Nile*
11. *The Purple Testament*
12. *The Big Tall Wish, I Am the Night-Color Me Black*
13. *Probe 7-Over and Out*
14. *A Hundred Yards Over the Rim*
15. *The Purple Testament, The 7th Is Made Up of Phantoms*
16. *The Parallel*
17. *The Bewitchin' Pool*
18. *The Trouble with Templeton*
19. *Printer's Devil*
20. *Of Late I Think of Cliffordville*
21. *The Lonely*
22. *A Most Unusual Camera*
23. *A Thing About Machines*
24. *A Hundred Yards Over the Rim*
25. *Judgment Night*
26. *The Four of Us are Dying, Death Ship*

Creature-Feature

1. Snake, centipede, spider
2. Raccoon
3. Mack
4. Rabbit's foot
5. Parrot
6. Attila
7. A giant red-eyed elephant
8. Three
9. Dinosaurs
10. Dead Goat

A World Of Possibilities

1. c
2. a
3. c
4. c

Kevin Bacon (7-degree)
Twilight Zone Thread
Part II

Animal House

John Belushi

The Blues Brothers

Ghostbusters

Stripes

Warren Oates

The Purple Testament

Cross Over Into . . . The Twilight Zone

Across	Down
1. Molly	1. McGarry
4. Ford	2. Light
6. Scissors	3. Year
9. Gig	4. Fatale
10. Teenya	5. Dan
11. Map	6. Shaver
12. Rot	7. Sam
13. Luck	8. Rip
15. Ellington	14. Klugman
20. Dane	16. Lady
22. UFO	17. Tuttle
23. Blue	18. Of
25. Dog	19. Nothing Human
26. Can	20. Denton
27. Grady	21. Noon
28. Tina	24. E.R.
32. Con	29. In
33. Eve	30. Ten
34. Alan	31. Mars
35. Sounds	32. Cat
37. Pen	35. Serling
38. With	36. Superstition
39. Hours	37. Pip
40. Pip	38. War
42. Mute	39. Houghton
43. Room	41. Hobo
44. JWB	42. Max
47. Big	44. JVP
49. Severed	45. We
51. Nothing	46. Brian
53. St.	48. It's
54. Anne	50. Dancing
55. Alter	52. Glades

58. Dingle	56. Rye
59. Ace	57. Food
60. Over	58. Die
61. Beluchi's	59. As
62. Sun	
63. God	

1 M	2 O	L	3 L	Y		4 F	O	R	5 D		6 S	C	I	S	7 S	O	R	8 S
C	I		E			A			A		H				A			I
9 G	I	G	A		10 T	E	E	N	Y	A			11 M	A	P			
A	H		R		A				A		V							
12 R	O	T			13 L	U	C	14 K		15 E	L	16 L	I	N	G	17 T	18 O	19 N
R		20 D	A	21 N	E			L		R		A				22 U	F	O
Y		E		O		23 B	L	U	24 E		25 D	O	G			T		T
	26 C	A	N	O			27 G	R	A	D	Y				30 T	T		H
		28 T	29 I	N	A			M					30 T		33 E	L		I
31 M		32 C	O	N				A					33 E	V	E			N
34 A	L	A	N		35 S	O	U	N	36 D	37 S		P	E	N				G
R		T			E			U		I			38 W	I	T	H		H
S			39 H	O	U	R	S		40 P	I	P		A					U
	41 H		O		L			42 M	U	T	E			43 R	O	O		M
	O		U		I			A		R		44 J	45 W	46 B				A
	47 B	48 I	G		N			X		49 S	E	V	E	R	E	50 D		N
51 N	O	T	H	I	N	G		52 G		T		P		I		A		
		53 S	T					L		I			54 A	N	N	E		
			O			55 A	L	T	E	R				C			57 F	
	58 D		N					D		I				I			O	
	I			59 A	C	E		60 O	V	E	R			N			O	
61 B	E	L	U	C	H	I	S		62 S	U	N				63 G	O	D	

ThirtySomething

1. d
2. a
3. c
4. d
5. d
6. c
7. d
8. d
9. b
10. f
11. b
12. e
13. 38

All Work And No Play

1. Model ships
2. 7 years
3. Hydrogen Armament
4. Hydro-electric
5. 13th floor
6. Specialties
7. Polodney's Books Store
8. Modern Science
9. Lifeguard
10. Treasures Unlimited
11. Ladies foundation garments
12. The New Life Corp.
13. Advertising agency, Executive
14. A drinking problem
15. Marty Sol
16. FAA
17. 17 years
18. Mr. Wilkenson
19. Carpentry
20. Design toys

Read All About It

1. *Printer's Devil*
2. *And When The Sky Was Opened*
3. *A Thing About Machines*
4. *King Nine Will Not Return*
5. *Time Enough At Last*
6. *Once Upon A Time*

Quote/Unquote In The Twilight Zone

1. *A Kind Of Stopwatch*
2. *The Grave*
3. *The Fugitive*
4. *The Bard*
5. *The Hunt*
6. *The Four Of Us Are Dying*
7. *In Praise Of Pip*
8. *Living Doll*
9. *A Stop At Willoughby*
10. *Static*
11. *The Dummy*
12. *Judgment Night*
13. *Elegy*

14. *The Sixteen Millimeter Shrine*
15. *A World Of Difference*
16. *It's A Good Life*
17. *The Trouble With Templeton*
18. *A Game Of Pool*
19. *The Hitchhiker*
20. *The Mirror*

Twilight Zone Fact or Fiction (Season One)

1. False (a comb)
2. False (nickel machine)
3. True
4. False ($1,000)
5. True
6. True
7. False (Wickwire)
8. False (Royal Flying Corps)
9. False (no receipt or refund)
10. True
11. True
12. False (Chicago)
13. True
14. True
15. True

Twilight Zone Fact or Fiction (Season Two)

1. False (7 years)
2. True
3. True

4. True
5. False (Jensen)
6. True
7. False (a new dress)
8. True
9. True
10. True
11. False (he was from Venus)
12. False (he wanted the lights on)
13. True
14. True
15. True

Twilight Zone Fact or Fiction (Season Three)

1. False (that's his favorite)
2. True
3. True
4. True
5. True
6. True
7. False ($200)
8. True
9. False (14/1 rack)
10. False (Sunnyvale Rest)
11. True
12. True
13. False (2 ft. Tall)
14. False (meteorology)
15. False (110 performances)

Twilight Zone Fact or Fiction (Season Four)

1. True
2. True
3. False (energy Field)
4. True
5. True
6. True
7. False (Homeville, Indiana)
8. False (perhaps a hammer in a dead seaman's hand)
9. True
10. False (Hermy was the last to run by Horace)
11. True
12. False
13. True
14. False (Coeurville)
15. True

Twilight Zone Fact or Fiction (Season Five)

1. False (cake)
2. True
3. True
4. True
5. True
6. True
7. False (they walked into it)
8. False (Hildy)
9. False (Boris)
10. True
11. True
12. False (they throw rocks at it)
13. False (3rd & Park)
14. False (administered free by his brother)
15. True

The Little People

1. Mr. Vance
2. Mr. Death
3. Patty
4. Miss Rogers
5. Ellen Tillman
6. Rocky Rhodes
7. Pete Grant
8. Les Goodman
9. Maya

Kevin Bacon (7-degree) Twilight Zone Thread Part III

JFK
My Cousin Vinnie
Ralph Machio
The Outsiders
Days of Thunder
Robert Duvall
Miniature

Made Up Of Phantoms

1. *It's A Good Life*
2. *Perchance To Dream*
3. *A World of His Own*
4. *What's In The Box*
5. *Walking Distance*
6. *The Last Flight*
7. *A Game of Pool*
8. *The Sixteen-Millimeter Shrine*
9. *The Bard*
10. *A Nice Place To Visit*
11. *Four 'O Clock*
12. *A Stop at Willoughby*
13. *It's A Good Life*
14. *Come Wander with Me*
15. *Will The Real Martian Please Stand Up?*

What You Need

1. d
2. c
3. j
4. e
5. g
6. b
7. i
8. a
9. h
10. f

The Invaders

1. Places
2. Cooking
3. Door
4. Blanket
5. Knife
6. Bed
7. Axe
8. USA
9. Giants
10. Gresham
11. Agnes Moorehead
12. Dialogue
13. Douglas Heyes
14. Richard Matheson

Still More Blankety-Blank Questions

1. loveliness
2. believe
3. sticksville
4. Love
5. ten
6. a hundred
7. dishes

And Now, Mr. Serling...

1. *The Invaders*
2. *Nightmare at 20,000 Feet*

3. *An Occurrence at Owl Creek Bridge*
4. *The Howling Man*
5. *The Midnight Sun*
6. *The Dummy*
7. *Night of the Meek*
8. *A Most Unusual Camera*
9. *Queen of the Nile*

Dèjá-View All Over Again

1. Victims of hit and run drivers
2. *The Bewitchin' Pool*
3. *The Fever, A Nice Place To Visit, Prime Mover*
4. *The Four of Us Are Dying, The Self Improvement of Salvadore Ross*
5. A fondness of hot Chocolate
6. *Elegy, On Thursday We Leave For Home, The Little People*
7. Jack Klugman & Mary Webster
8. *Uncle Simon, The Brain Center at Whipple's*

The Chaser Pt VII

1. grapefruit juice
2. *A Quality of Mercy*
3. *Passage on The Lady Anne*
4. Harrington, Forbes, Gart
5. 247 lbs.
6. Club Bonanza
7. An antique touring car
8. 3 times
9. *The Obsolete Man*
10. The Miller boys
11. Ira the bartender
12. 14 years
13. 1:15
14. Burton County Museum
15. *Elegy*
16. 8
17. Fast Gun Developer
18. Jack's Fix-It Shop
19. Anne Marie Mitchell
20. Linotype Operator

Where Is Everybody?

H	A	N	P	N	O	I	S	N	E	M	I	D	H	T	F	I	F	A	J	S
T	I	U	S	D	V	O	P	S	R	U	N	N	S	T	U	U	Z	A	D	A
I	T	T	R	T	A	F	A	F	T	E	R	H	O	U	R	S	R	D	E	Y
H	T	C	V	V	A	B	R	A	P	A	S	S	A	N	R	U	O	E	B
E	D	Q	U	H	G	E	Z	D	O	D	N	O	P	D	E	S	I	L	N	H
U	S	A	R	T	H	G	O	P	O	R	H	U	A	N	T	E	K	L	A	G
Q	T	O	L	O	J	I	P	W	D	V	O	M	R	D	E	A	T	H	B	U
U	I	D	L	A	D	B	K	G	O	A	B	P	D	I	L	O	P	A	P	O
P	M	D	O	W	O	S	Y	E	C	H	N	I	W	R	O	C	Z	O	N	L
D	E	M	N	V	O	M	E	E	R	D	J	P	D	A	S	I	L	V	R	L
R	O	D	D	Z	P	O	R	R	Z	O	N	D	A	R	B	E	M	I	S	I
E	H	W	T	H	E	T	W	I	L	I	G	H	T	Z	O	N	E	W	P	W
A	H	P	R	J	L	O	O	P	N	I	H	C	T	I	W	E	B	T	S	R
M	A	I	U	Q	U	S	T	I	M	A	N	A	K	A	G	J	L	D	G	G
P	I	N	M	A	A	C	N	U	S	T	H	G	I	N	D	I	M	O	D	D
N	Y	A	P	C	T	E	M	P	L	E	T	O	N	B	R	I	R	E	N	D
J	A	M	E	S	O	N	S	E	M	E	K	N	D	P	Y	Q	N	I	N	O
M	D	O	T	D	B	Z	A	T	L	E	V	J	O	Y	X	V	R	G	A	O
F	S	V	U	D	E	I	L	G	N	I	L	W	O	H	S	I	Z	T	L	W
S	M	E	C	V	H	O	N	N	B	Z	X	D	F	K	L	S	G	S	E	E
D	O	E	S	D	X	A	W	U	G	L	C	I	N	V	A	D	E	R	S	M
G	O	V	F	G	R	Z	F	O	Y	K	A	A	K	M	J	W	H	Y	I	O
A	D	A	R	C	O	R	N	F	I	E	L	D	E	L	E	T	Z	O	N	H

The After Hours

E	L	B	M	I	H	T	T	H	E	P	P	I	M
M	R	S	A	R	L	A	T	E	G	A	H	S	A
I	O	T	M	A	R	L	N	N	Q	D	I	I	N
N	O	A	N	B	D	L	I	L	I	E	O	C	N
L	L	Y	A	A	A	L	S	O	H	H	U	N	N
E	F	L	O	F	R	F	O	P	T	C	R	A	O
R	H	O	L	E	O	M	P	G	T	T	S	R	O
L	T	O	S	S	A	D	B	L	H	A	S	F	L
P	N	P	M	O	T	H	E	R	G	R	H	E	F
L	I	L	Z	E	E	H	T	A	U	C	S	N	S
G	N	M	O	A	Z	E	T	Z	G	S	Q	N	I
O	T	R	N	T	T	I	U	Q	S	M	T	A	N
L	S	N	I	U	Q	E	N	N	A	M	U	E	A
E	T	H	T	N	O	M	E	N	O	Y	O	U	R
R	O	O	L	F	D	R	I	H	T	F	O	R	B

Vera, Vera, Mirror, Mirror

M	I	L	E	Z	O	N	A	T	Z	M	C	A	R
C	A	L	H	E	R	S	E	L	F	I	I	L	O
C	U	R	C	I	H	J	U	I	S	S	U	Q	D
R	O	S	T	M	I	L	S	B	E	O	J	U	A
S	E	R	Z	I	Y	Y	L	L	U	T	U	I	E
E	A	V	T	A	N	T	I	L	T	R	I	L	T
G	W	L	T	L	O	M	O	M	V	R	C	O	S
A	O	I	T	B	A	L	I	I	T	I	E	A	N
G	C	G	T	R	L	N	E	L	L	M	J	I	I
G	G	H	E	H	O	L	D	L	N	U	D	G	R
Y	A	V	A	M	J	C	T	I	L	E	Q	H	G
S	B	T	S	A	F	U	Z	O	T	A	R	T	L
P	G	A	R	T	U	C	I	A	R	F	R	L	U
E	S	A	C	F	E	I	R	B	U	A	L	A	A
S	I	S	H	E	R	S	E	L	F	S	O	P	P

Please Stand Up!

A	B	O	S	H	K	Q	T	O	A	R	M	S	L	U
S	D	R	O	M	S	U	N	K	J	I	R	M	H	L
X	N	I	I	O	L	R	C	J	S	E	L	W	V	L
O	P	G	R	D	O	L	U	G	P	I	D	K	H	V
B	O	Q	O	P	G	N	F	O	E	H	A	J	J	E
E	D	U	E	B	O	E	O	L	F	Y	B	M	I	N
K	W	I	J	W	B	R	L	O	G	B	R	O	X	U
U	S	E	N	Q	T	G	E	B	K	L	E	O	E	S
J	N	I	P	F	O	M	L	V	O	T	C	K	S	D
E	A	I	T	S	R	J	K	A	I	E	N	X	I	S
D	G	A	L	I	A	C	B	S	K	R	A	F	N	E
T	T	H	G	X	B	C	E	S	U	T	D	P	N	G
S	N	F	Y	B	D	Y	O	U	O	X	O	S	T	A
A	F	H	E	C	E	O	B	O	X	N	O	G	U	A
M	A	R	T	I	A	N	L	K	O	Z	E	L	O	B

The Eye Of The Beholder

C	O	N	F	O	R	M	I	T	Y	E	L	O	P	X	I	N	D	E
E	Y	B	E	H	T	X	Z	A	G	F	T	H	E	E	Y	C	L	D
M	P	T	G	D	A	L	L	A	W	E	R	N	O	S	A	E	R	T
A	O	T	H	E	B	L	D	D	E	L	K	D	R	V	A	A	O	E
X	L	E	G	E	A	N	E	O	F	Z	Y	R	M	E	K	P	W	M
E	R	B	H	R	A	M	L	O	N	O	T	B	T	N	I	S	I	A
S	F	E	E	B	E	A	L	G	D	N	U	R	T	L	N	H	D	E
K	H	A	T	G	Y	X	I	W	L	S	A	E	H	E	T	A	E	R
A	Y	D	J	E	P	Z	H	R	I	U	E	D	R	D	O	D	C	G
E	C	E	O	S	R	O	I	A	T	S	B	R	O	E	O	F	O	N
R	B	A	M	G	E	N	L	S	Y	E	S	N	E	U	N	A	O	I
F	S	R	P	N	T	I	E	P	H	C	A	E	E	R	G	C	P	L
I	O	H	I	I	Y	N	L	L	J	N	S	A	N	S	I	L	L	R
N	T	N	L	P	I	T	B	P	E	D	O	R	O	K	G	E	A	E
O	L	M	S	X	T	W	I	G	Z	V	N	D	S	P	R	H	N	S
L	D	I	A	E	Y	I	G	H	O	S	E	I	E	E	H	A	E	C
M	I	M	L	E	S	E	R	B	A	L	A	N	C	E	T	I	D	S

Walking Distance

D	N	O	S	L	I	W	R	M	O	N	K	W	O	N	K	L	S	P
A	A	E	B	E	N	I	U	J	J	S	E	I	K	O	A	U	Q	O
H	E	M	O	M	I	G	D	E	K	O	O	L	X	P	M	D	U	L
S	L	I	R	O	R	G	T	G	J	E	B	D	O	M	G	D	I	H
A	E	C	P	R	O	N	Y	G	H	A	M	O	E	I	G	C	P	Y
L	I	R	Y	I	M	Q	D	H	O	T	R	R	S	I	I	H	O	H
F	M	E	V	N	U	P	R	O	M	T	A	N	Y	N	E	O	O	O
Y	T	S	R	I	O	O	E	M	E	L	H	N	Y	E	Z	C	K	M
E	S	O	E	G	C	S	G	E	W	Q	T	A	B	V	C	O	L	M
P	I	T	R	G	S	F	L	R	O	U	I	C	B	E	L	L	I	O
T	D	L	O	L	A	L	R	O	I	G	F	O	L	E	A	W	N
H	R	S	S	B	D	B	A	N	D	C	O	N	C	E	R	T	S	P
A	A	J	M	G	R	B	I	Y	Z	K	W	F	U	O	I	E	O	L
N	M	U	U	I	O	T	B	G	L	N	E	A	B	O	Z	C	N	P
A	R	G	Q	J	R	C	O	R	I	O	V	R	E	O	Y	I	R	M
W	A	L	T	A	L	E	L	O	W	A	I	Y	R	O	H	G	B	I
N	M	O	M	I	M	H	G	D	T	Z	R	D	T	K	C	U	I	L
M	A	R	S	E	S	N	E	C	I	L	S	R	E	V	I	R	D	G

Death Ship

P	I	D	N	O	S	S	U	C	R	A	M	A	G	R	O	P
Z	H	A	P	L	R	E	V	R	A	F	L	A	N	S	E	R
E	O	A	D	I	A	D	E	K	A	L	B	O	T	G	B	D
N	M	A	R	Q	W	I	A	S	E	Y	T	B	K	I	D	E
I	F	B	K	R	U	T	D	N	N	K	S	C	H	A	L	C
M	A	T	R	Y	I	A	J	I	C	S	T	O	S	R	E	K
I	S	T	I	Y	B	N	A	P	O	N	E	E	G	C	I	E
J	A	R	S	L	O	R	G	R	Z	A	B	R	I	K	F	R
L	C	A	N	D	C	O	H	T	Z	R	O	S	L	R	S	W
O	G	G	A	S	R	E	N	N	O	C	L	I	S	A	N	I
D	I	M	B	M	M	A	B	F	A	N	N	Q	U	H	A	O
O	A	K	M	N	E	N	O	Z	C	E	J	I	M	I	T	N
R	D	A	C	O	N	R	A	D	F	S	E	B	N	A	S	P

A Most Unusual Camera

T	W	I	G	H	S	O	I	R	U	C	A	L
O	C	A	H	U	M	A	N	I	T	Y	S	R
G	A	A	B	L	U	P	A	P	A	N	D	O
E	N	Q	M	D	R	A	W	D	O	O	W	N
R	E	U	S	E	T	U	H	I	G	L	W	O
E	J	E	A	G	R	L	T	D	L	R	A	S
T	A	W	A	N	F	A	W	T	F	O	U	R
I	P	E	L	L	T	L	E	I	A	E	H	A
A	H	I	H	I	T	N	O	D	R	M	G	C
W	G	G	P	O	L	U	T	T	E	A	T	N
H	I	L	C	R	O	I	K	O	T	C	O	A
M	A	W	A	L	D	K	L	W	S	V	N	E
P	O	H	S	Y	E	C	O	N	E	A	I	J
A	D	S	T	S	U	M	P	T	H	S	E	S
C	L	W	T	Y	Y	T	A	O	C	R	U	F
H	O	O	D	S	U	R	E	I	U	Q	Q	U
G	I	R	P	G	N	I	L	R	E	S	T	R

The Four Of Us . . .

G	F	A	K	R	G	I	R	E	T	S	B	O	L	A
I	L	H	M	F	I	A	J	F	E	B	P	Y	C	E
K	M	A	G	A	N	G	S	T	E	R	I	O	I	D
S	J	U	C	B	H	T	N	C	X	E	L	G	I	R
I	G	U	S	S	G	T	E	O	D	A	G	Z	Z	O
H	I	G	D	I	E	F	A	P	A	A	L	Y	O	M
I	Q	U	A	R	C	H	H	A	M	M	E	R	H	A
J	G	D	E	O	A	I	K	P	G	U	N	O	L	R
L	U	X	U	R	O	P	A	X	X	M	R	U	S	S
P	O	A	R	H	F	B	C	N	K	P	A	T	H	H
B	I	S	V	N	H	W	G	W	G	Z	V	N	M	A
O	T	F	M	G	N	I	Y	D	I	H	L	S	T	K
U	P	U	L	S	F	O	S	T	E	R	T	M	U	B

The Invaders

E	E	A	T	W	I	L	H	J	U	Q	U	S	A	S
X	D	E	A	H	M	B	O	N	F	E	E	A	L	T
A	P	O	O	A	L	R	A	O	L	B	L	M	O	N
G	G	H	T	R	A	E	H	S	O	E	E	L	P	A
I	G	N	G	P	L	A	C	E	S	E	A	D	L	I
A	B	K	E	C	Z	D	A	H	K	G	R	O	Y	G
B	G	O	E	S	O	I	R	T	I	S	O	P	T	H
F	N	R	N	F	M	T	S	A	R	T	O	O	Y	T
D	S	L	E	I	N	O	M	M	D	S	B	T	W	Z
I	F	L	O	S	E	K	O	D	G	I	L	Q	I	O
A	X	A	O	N	H	L	W	R	H	M	A	U	L	S
L	Z	E	R	Q	P	A	E	A	E	P	N	O	G	E
O	U	V	F	U	L	A	M	H	O	H	K	P	R	C
G	O	G	N	I	K	O	O	C	S	L	E	O	O	S
U	P	L	R	T	N	C	T	I	T	E	T	A	O	E
E	R	O	R	W	Q	K	S	R	H	S	F	O	D	A
S	D	V	A	I	U	J	P	C	W	O	O	L	N	F
S	E	Y	E	H	S	A	L	G	U	O	D	K	A	K

BearManorMedia

Can you resist looking at these great titles from Bearmanor Media?

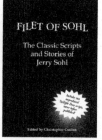

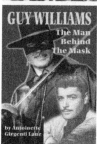

We didn't think so.

To get details on these, and nearly a hundred more titles—visit

www.bearmanormedia.com

You'll be sorry!

...if you miss out.   P.S. Don't be sorry.

CPSIA information can be obtained at www.ICGtesting.com
Printed in the USA
BVOW08s0239290515

402029BV00009B/365/P

9 781593 931360